BLAIRSVILLE SENIOR HIGH SCHOOL
BLAIRSVILLE, PENNA.

AMERICA the BEAUTIFUL
MONTANA

By Ann Heinrichs

Consultants

Michael P. Malone, Vice President for Academic Affairs, Montana State University, Bozeman

David Walter, Research Director, Montana Historical Society

Merrill G. Burlingame, Ph.D., D.HL., Professor Emeritus, Montana State University, Bozeman

Robert L. Hillerich, Ph.D., Bowling Green State University, Bowling Green, Ohio

CHILDRENS PRESS®
CHICAGO

Warren Peak in the Anaconda-Pintler Wilderness

Project Editor: Joan Downing
Associate Editor: Shari Joffe
Design Director: Margrit Fiddle
Typesetting: Graphic Connections, Inc.
Engraving: Liberty Photoengraving

Library of Congress Cataloging-in-Publication Data

Heinrichs, Ann.
    America the beautiful. Montana / by Ann
Heinrichs.
        p.   cm.
    Includes index.
    Summary: Introduces the geography, history,
government, economy, industry, culture, historic
sites, and famous people of Montana.
    ISBN 0-516-00472-7
    1. Montana—Juvenile literature.
[1. Montana] I. Title.
F731.3.H45   1991   90-21035
    978.6—dc20   CIP
                                              AC

Fishing along the Madison River

TABLE OF CONTENTS

Chapter 1

MONTANA,
THE LAST BEST PLACE

MONTANA, THE LAST BEST PLACE

The Last Best Place, the Treasure State, Big Sky Country—
Montana's many nicknames give away its secret.

From the rugged wilds of the western mountains to the stark
skyline of the eastern plains, Montana is one of the last vast,
uncluttered spots in the nation. There are more deer, elk,
antelopes, and bears in Montana than there are people.

Yet, over the years, the beautiful land of Montana has been
flooded by wave after wave of human invasion. Fur traders fought
over it and gold rushers overran it. For the area's Native
Americans, who had lived there for centuries, the land would
never be the same. By the end of the 1800s, the infamous "copper
kings" controlled much of the state. Copper and coal mining
stripped some areas bare.

Finally, ecology-minded Montanans called a halt to the raids.
Aggressive laws were passed to preserve the landscape, tax the
mineral companies, and repair a century of plunder. Ironically,
Montana now faces new invasions. Tourists arrive in record
numbers, and out-of-staters buy up choice parcels of land.

Montana remains split between those who want to open the
doors and those who prefer to keep the state a secret. Either way,
visitors who respect Montana's natural splendors are met with
frank hospitality. In the words of Montana artist Charlie Russell,
"My brother, when you come to my lodge, the robe will be spread
and the pipe of peace will be lit."

Chapter 2
THE LAND

THE LAND

Montana's diverse terrain was formed over millions of years by dramatic volcanic eruptions and clashing upheavals of land. Shallow seas covered the land from time to time, and great ice sheets gouged out basins and smoothed the plains.

GEOGRAPHY

With an area of 147,046 square miles (380,849 square kilometers), Montana is the fourth-largest of all the states. Only Alaska, Texas, and California have greater land areas. Montana is also the largest among the Rocky Mountain states, a grouping that includes Idaho, Nevada, Utah, Colorado, and Wyoming.

From west to east, Montana measures 559 miles (900 kilometers) at its widest point. North to south, its greatest distance is 321 miles (517 kilometers). Nearly rectangular in shape, the state has a jagged western and southwestern border that winds and twists through the mountaintops. The southwestern portion of this border runs along the Continental Divide, a chain of mountain peaks that separates North America's westward- and eastward-flowing rivers.

The state of Idaho shares Montana's irregular western border, and Idaho and Wyoming lie along its southern edge. Montana is bordered on the east by North Dakota and South Dakota. On the north, Montana is bordered by the Canadian provinces of British Columbia, Alberta, and Saskatchewan.

The Absaroka-Beartooth Wilderness (left) and Kootenai National Forest (right) lie in Montana's Rocky Mountain region.

TOPOGRAPHY

Montana straddles both the Rocky Mountain and the Great Plains regions of the United States. The western two-fifths of the state is Montana's Rocky Mountain zone, where forested hillsides slope down from lofty peaks to fertile, green valleys. Lumbering, mining, farming, and tourism thrive in these western mountains. Rich mineral deposits here have given Montana the nickname "Treasure State."

The Rocky Mountain ranges that lie in Montana generally run northwest to southeast. They include the Cabinet, Bitterroot, Salish, Sapphire, Mission, and Swan ranges. Farther east, toward the center of the state, are the Big Belt and Little Belt mountains.

Glacier National Park, in northeastern Montana, adjoins Canada's Waterton Lakes National Park. Together, the two parks

Above: Mount Wilbur in Glacier National Park
Right: A wheat field in north-central Montana

form Waterton-Glacier International Peace Park, a wonderland of glaciers, streams, valleys, and peaks. A small section of Yellowstone National Park, most of which lies in Wyoming, reaches into south-central Montana. The Absaroka, Beartooth, Pryor, and Rosebud mountains run along Montana's southern border. Just north of Yellowstone Park is Granite Peak, the state's highest point, standing 12,799 feet (3,901 meters) high.

Montana's Great Plains region covers the eastern three-fifths of the state. Here, endless stretches of rangeland and gently rolling plains seem to draw the eye upward toward Montana's spacious skies. This awesome vista has given Montana another nickname, the "Big Sky Country." Herds of cattle graze on Montana's high plains, and wheat fields wave in the wind. The state's best farmland lies in two areas of the Great Plains: along the Yellowstone River Valley and in the "Golden Triangle" region of north-central Montana.

Above: Bighorn Canyon, in south-central Montana

Jutting up from the plains are several small mountain ranges, including the Bears Paw, Judith, Little Rocky, Highwood, and Crazy mountains. In far-eastern Montana is an eerie badlands region, an arid expanse of eroded soil dotted with bizarre sandstone buttes and red rock masses.

RIVERS AND LAKES

The Missouri and the Yellowstone are Montana's most important rivers. Together, they drain about 85 percent of the state's land area. Both rise in the western mountains, flowing eastward until they join just east of the Montana-North Dakota border. From its source at the juncture of the Madison, Jefferson, and Gallatin rivers, the Missouri follows a great northerly arc past Helena and Great Falls. On its eastward course, it widens into Fort Peck Lake, formed by Fort Peck Dam. The Missouri's major

St. Mary Lake is one of hundreds of lakes scattered throughout Glacier National Park.

tributaries include the Sun, Teton, Marias, Musselshell, and Milk rivers.

The Yellowstone rises in Yellowstone National Park and flows across the southern part of the state. The Yellowstone's tributaries include the Stillwater, Bighorn, Rosebud, Tongue, and Powder rivers. In western Montana, the Clark Fork of the Columbia River is the major waterway. The Blackfoot, Bitterroot, and Flathead rivers are the Clark Fork's major branches.

Flathead Lake, in northwestern Montana, is the state's largest natural lake. It is also the largest natural freshwater lake west of the Mississippi River. Hundreds of other glacial lakes are scattered in and around Glacier National Park. Montana's largest artificial lake is Fort Peck Lake. Other lakes created by damming rivers are Hungry Horse Reservoir, Bighorn Lake, Tiber Reservoir, and Canyon Ferry Lake. Lake Koocanusa, formed by Libby Dam on the Kootenai River, extends into British Columbia.

CLIMATE

Montana's two contrasting land regions create wildly differing weather conditions. West of the Continental Divide, the climate is generally more temperate and the precipitation (moisture such as rain and snow) is heavier. The divide protects the western region from severe Canadian winds and also captures the moisture from Pacific Ocean breezes.

In January, temperatures west of the Continental Divide average 20 degrees Fahrenheit (minus 7 degrees Celsius), while the January average in the eastern part of the state is 14 degrees Fahrenheit (minus 10 degrees Celsius). Temperatures in July average 64 degrees Fahrenheit (18 degrees Celsius) in the western mountains and 71 degrees Fahrenheit (22 degrees Celsius) in the east. Two eastern Montana towns, Glendive and Medicine Lake, reached the state's highest recorded temperature of 117 degrees Fahrenheit (47 degrees Celsius). Glendive set the record on July 20, 1893, and Medicine Lake matched it on July 5, 1937.

Severe blizzards visit the eastern plains in the winter, and fierce winds from Canada whip down across the highlands. However, warm, dry winter winds called *chinooks* also gust down from the eastern slopes of the Continental Divide. The lowest temperature ever recorded in Montana was minus 70 degrees Fahrenheit (minus 57 degrees Celsius), at Rogers Pass on January 20, 1954. Although temperatures are more extreme in the east, the drier air makes them less uncomfortable.

Montana's heaviest rains fall in the spring and early summer, and the heaviest snowfall occurs in the mountains. Excluding the far west, Montana's average precipitation statewide is 13 to 14 inches (33 to 36 centimeters) a year. More than 34 inches (86 centimeters) of moisture falls on Heron, in the far northwest.

ANIMAL AND PLANT LIFE

Thousands of buffalo, or bison, once ranged across Montana's plains. While Indians hunted them to provide for life's necessities, white settlers hunted them for sport until they were nearly extinct. A herd of about four hundred buffalo is now protected near Moiese on the National Bison Range, established in 1908.

Elk, mule deer, white-tailed deer, moose, pronghorn antelope, black bears, grizzly bears, mountain goats, and mountain sheep are some of Montana's other large mammals. Most live in the mountainous areas, although deer and pronghorns can be seen on the plains. Predatory animals in Montana's forests and mountains include coyotes, lynxes, mountain lions, and wolves. Some of the state's smaller animals are beavers, foxes, muskrats, weasels, martens, mink, and otters.

Around three hundred types of birds inhabit the state, including bobolinks, chickadees, magpies, meadowlarks, vultures, and hawks. Magpies have a habit of strolling on the backs of grazing animals in search of succulent insects. Among Montana's game birds are pheasants, partridges, grouse, and various species of ducks and geese. Rare trumpeter swans inhabit Red Rock Lakes National Wildlife Refuge.

Many kinds of lizards and snakes live in Montana, but the state's only poisonous reptile is the rattlesnake. A rare salamander, the axolotl (Mexican Spanish for "plays in the water"), lives in the lakes and pools of southwestern Montana.

Trout and grayling abound in the lakes and streams. More than seventy other kinds of fish live in the state, including salmon, pike, sturgeon, crappie, whitefish, and perch.

About one-fourth of Montana is covered with forest. Most of this forestland is in the west. Cone-bearing trees include Douglas

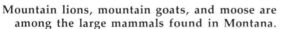

Mountain lions, mountain goats, and moose are among the large mammals found in Montana.

firs, cedars, larches, spruces, hemlocks, and pines. Ashes, alders, aspens, birches, cottonwoods, and willows are some of the state's deciduous (leaf-bearing) trees.

Various grasses carpet Montana's mountain valleys. Blue grama and needlegrass, as well as sagebrush and cactus, grow on the broad plains. Colorful wildflowers such as asters, bluebells, Indian paintbrushes, poppies, and primroses brighten Montana's scenic panoramas.

Both state and federal laws protect much of Montana's wildlife and wilderness. Bald eagle, grizzly bear, and gray wolf populations, once declining at an alarming rate, have rebounded in recent years. Environmentalists in the state are constantly battling mining and agricultural interests, tourism and recreation industries, and electric power utilities to preserve Montana's natural wealth.

Chapter 3
THE PEOPLE

THE PEOPLE

Montanans, though scattered widely across the state, are linked together by common bonds. Their turbulent history and their love for the land seem to bridge all distances.

POPULATION

According to the United States Census Bureau, Montana's 1990 population was 799,065. This ranked Montana forty-fourth among the states in number of residents. Only Delaware, Vermont, North Dakota, South Dakota, Wyoming, and Alaska had fewer people. In 1985, the state's population reached a peak, at 826,000 residents, but declined to about 806,000 in 1989.

With such a small population in the nation's fourth-largest state, there is plenty of elbow room in the Big Sky Country. On average, there are only 5.5 Montanans per square mile (2 per square kilometer), compared to the national average of 70 people per square mile (27 people per square kilometer).

Compared to urban areas in most other states, Montana's cities are small. According to the 1990 census, Billings is the state's largest city, with a population of 81,151. Next, in descending order of size, are Great Falls, Missoula, Butte, Helena, and Bozeman. For a state capital, Helena is quite small. The census bureau counted only 24,569 residents in 1990. Some 40 percent of state's total population lives in the ten largest cities.

Montana's pioneer heritage is preserved at the Big Horn County Historical Museum in Hardin.

Since the 1950s, droves of new residents have migrated to the West for its climate, relaxed lifestyle, and wide-open spaces. Montana, however, is one of the slowest-growing of the western states. Between 1980 and 1990, its population grew only 1.6 percent, while the population of the United States as a whole grew 9.8 percent.

POPULATION DISTRIBUTION

Montana has two official metropolitan areas. The Billings metropolitan area extends over much of Yellowstone County, while the Great Falls metropolitan area encompasses Cascade County. Within these two areas live 21 percent of the state's residents. During the 1970s, Yellowstone County's population grew a whopping 24 percent, and in the 1980s, grew another 5 percent. The Great Falls metropolitan area, on the other hand, was the only one in the West to shrink between 1970 and 1980. Its population dropped just over 1 percent, and that decline continued in the 1980s.

In the 1880s, a mining boom brought a 265 percent increase in population to Montana. The urban population in that same decade grew an amazing 455 percent. Each new mineral strike drew hundreds of fortune hunters, who then organized formal towns. Butte, Helena, and many other Montana cities started out as mining-camp towns. It was not until the 1950s, though, that Montana's city residents outnumbered its rural population. Today, about 53 percent of Montanans live in cities and towns, while the rest are spread out beneath the Big Sky.

A STATE OF DIVERSITY

Most of Montana's gold rushers were people originally from the midwestern and eastern United States who had come West to reap the mineral riches of California, Colorado, Nevada, or Idaho. A later copper-mining boom attracted miners from Germany, Ireland, Wales, and England's Cornwall region. Coal mines drew Italians and Scots. Scandinavians, eastern Europeans, and more Germans settled in farming communities throughout the state. In 1980, one out of every six Montanans was born outside the United States. Most of these immigrants came from Canada, Germany, or Norway.

Scattered around Montana today are pockets of ethnic groups that have preserved their cultural heritages. Dozens of colonies of Hutterites, a communal German religious group that arrived in the early 1900s, are located near Lewistown and other communities. Near Missoula is a settlement of Laotian Hmong people. So many nationalities settled in the mining town of Red Lodge that the community hosts an annual Festival of Nations to honor each of them.

About 93 percent of Montanans are white, while whites make up 80 percent of the nation as a whole. About 12 thousand Hispanics—less than 2 percent of the state's population—live in Montana. Many came to Montana in the 1920s to work the sugar-beet fields. Mining camps once drew many black workers to Montana. Today, about two thousand African Americans live in Montana.

MONTANA'S INDIANS

More than forty-eight thousand people, or about 6 percent of the state's total population, belong to one of Montana's ten American Indian groups. They are concentrated in seven reservation areas, although many Indian families live outside the reservations.

In the northwest, the Flathead Reservation is home to the confederated Salish (who were called the Flathead by early Europeans) and Kootenai groups. Piegan Blackfeet live on the Blackfeet Reservation surrounding Browning. Gros Ventre and Assiniboine people reside on the Fort Belknap Reservation. Assiniboine also occupy the Fort Peck Reservation in the northeast, along with the Sioux. Northern Cheyenne reside on the Northern Cheyenne Reservation around Lame Deer, and Crow Indians live on the Crow Reservation south of Hardin. Chippewa and Cree Indians, whose ancestors arrived in the 1880s and later, occupy the Rocky Boy's Indian Reservation near Havre.

The Northern Cheyenne Indian Reservation is one of seven Indian reservations in Montana.

Montana's Indians draw profits from mining, lumbering, fishing, hunting, and grazing activities on their lands. Tribal councils elect their own leaders and oversee education, law enforcement, and economic affairs for their tribes. Occasionally, representatives from all groups meet to discuss matters that concern them all.

POLITICS

Montana is definitely a two-party state. Most of Montana's territorial governors were Republicans. Between 1889 and 1940, however, all but two of Montana's governors were Democrats. Since then, voters have chosen a fairly even mix of Republican and Democratic governors. Throughout the 1970s, Democrats controlled the state legislature. In 1981, for the first time in ten years, Republican legislators slipped into the majority.

Because America's population is always shifting, the 435 seats of the United States House of Representatives are redivided among the states after each census. In the 1980s, Montana had two United States representatives. In the 1990s, however, Montana lost one of its seats, because its population growth during the previous decade had been less than that of many other states.

Montana voters swing toward the Republicans in presidential elections. Except for 1964, when they sided with Democrat Lyndon Johnson, Montanans have supported the Republican presidential candidate in every election after 1948.

RELIGION

Montana's first ministers were a handful of Jesuit priests who ministered to the Salish Indians. Later, Methodist, Baptist, Presbyterian, and Episcopalian ministers arrived to preach to the gold rushers. These fiery "brimstone busters" held forth wherever they found a crowd—which was often in saloons, dance halls, and roulette joints.

It is difficult to make an accurate estimate of Montanans' religious affiliations today. Most of the state's people belong to various Christian faiths. The largest group is Roman Catholics, who make up about 17 percent of the population. The Methodist and Lutheran denominations also have sizable followings. Other religious adherents include Presbyterians, Congregationalists, Baptists, and Disciples of Christ. Membership in the Church of Jesus Christ of Latter-day Saints, also called the Mormon church, is increasing rapidly. Jewish people number less than 1 percent of Montana's population. A large number of evangelical Christian groups have formed in recent years.

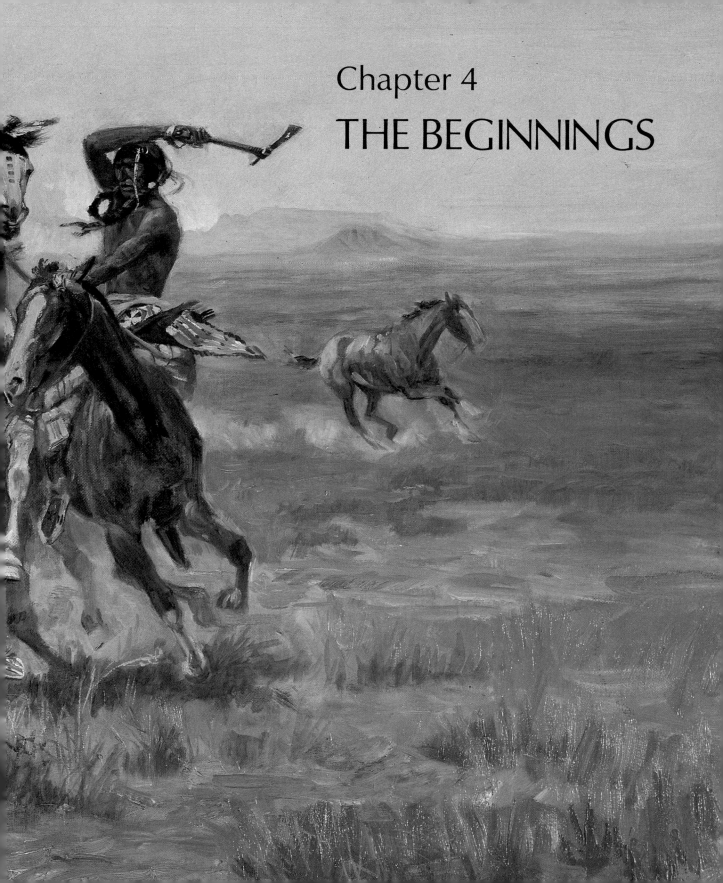

Chapter 4
THE BEGINNINGS

THE BEGINNINGS

Millions of years ago, swamps and tropical forests covered what is now Montana. Gigantic dinosaurs such as the Triceratops, the Stegosaurus, and the fierce Tyrannosaurus Rex roamed the land. In the waters lurked monstrous ichthyosaurs, plesiosaurs, and armored sharks. Earthquakes or tons of ash from erupting volcanoes may have made these beasts extinct. The only records of their existence throughout Montana are their fossil remains.

Long after the dinosaurs were gone, Montana's earliest mammals appeared. Across the land ranged mammoths, camels, elephants, bison, giant horses, and giant sloths. A fifty-thousand-year-old mammoth skull found in the Yellowstone Valley gives an indication of these creatures' size. Its tusks alone are 18 feet (5 meters) long.

EARLY PEOPLES

As early as forty thousand years ago, human beings first entered North America pursuing those very animals. These early hunters probably crossed what is now the Bering Strait from present-day Siberia to Alaska. From there, they gradually spread over the continent as they hunted animals for food and clothing.

The earliest people known to have lived in Montana are called the Folsom people. Folsom remains found near Helena, around Medicine Lake, and at other sites reveal what little is known of them. Living at least ten thousand years ago, the Folsom people

This painting by Charles M. Russell depicts Montana before the arrival of Europeans, when thousands of bison roamed freely across the plains.

used a sling called an *atlatl* to hurl stone-pointed darts and spears at prehistoric bison.

About seven thousand years ago, as the huge game animals were vanishing, people of the Yuma culture began to appear in Montana. Yuma people were the first Montanans known to have inhabited the far-western mountains. Their mysterious pictographs, or picture writings, can be seen at Pictograph Cave east of Billings, in the Three Forks and West Yellowstone areas, and throughout the Rocky Mountain region. These mysterious drawings of men and women, animals, and strange emblems were made to record events or to call upon spiritual forces in nature. Yuma people foraged for roots, berries, and seeds, and hunted rabbits and other small game. They roasted roots in pits, ground seeds into flour, and baked on stone hearths.

About three thousand years ago, the period of Montana's Late Hunters began. These people hunted elk, deer, and, most importantly, buffalo. The buffalo provided not only meat, but also clothing, shelter, and tools. Buffalo hides were made into moccasins and leggings. Skins wrapped around a circle of leaning poles made a cone-shaped tent. Hooves provided glue, shoulder bones became axes and hoes, horns were used as spoons, and the stomach lining could be used as a bucket. A woolly buffalo pelt made a warm bed, and buffalo skins stretched over a wood frame provided a boat.

For the Late Hunters, buffalo hunting was a fine art. Throughout Montana, hundreds of sites called buffalo cliffs, buffalo jump sites, or *pishkuns* reveal the Late Hunters' buffalo-hunting technique. The hunters would arrange stones in a V-shaped pattern that led to the edge of a cliff. Then they would drive a herd of buffalo into a stampede within the V until the animals, unable to stop, plummeted over the edge.

NATIVE GROUPS

Distinct groups of prehistoric Montana natives cannot be clearly identified. Many had religious ceremonies during the summer solstice, the longest day of the year, to honor the sun or the sky gods. Some groups engaged in warfare with others. Some had secret societies for warriors, with many levels, from young to very old and experienced. After horses were introduced in the 1700s, people of the plains hunted on horseback. When white explorers first reached Montana and began to make written records of what they observed, they encountered several distinct groups of Indians.

In the western mountain region were the Salish, Kalispel, Kootenai, and Shoshone. They fished the mountain streams, trapped small game, and gathered bitterroot, camas, wild carrots, and other roots. The Salish lived in the Flathead Lake area and the Bitterroot Valley. The Kootenai, who ranged from northwest

Montana through northern Idaho and into Canada, hunted deer and tanned their hides. Their birchbark canoes resembled those of some Siberian peoples.

Across the Great Plains ranged the Blackfeet, Crow, Assiniboine, Cheyenne, and Atsina. The Plains Indians hunted buffalo and other game. They gathered wild turnips and other roots, picked berries, and made pemmican, a dried-meat food. Other groups, such as the Bannock and the Sioux, often hunted in Montana.

EARLY EUROPEAN EXPLORATION

Many early explorations of the American West were spurred by the quest for a Northwest Passage—a water route through North America to the Pacific Ocean. Trappers and traders penetrated the western wilderness as well, charting trails never recorded before.

Historians are not certain which white people were the first to tread on Montana soil. Most believe that two brothers, François and Louis Joseph de La Vérendrye, were the first to arrive. Their father Pierre, a French trader, had sent them off to verify an Indian tale of a river that flowed into a western sea. On January 1, 1743, the two brothers spotted what they called "shining mountains." They could not record their exact whereabouts because they had broken their astrolabe, a location-finding instrument. However, the shining peaks are believed to have been the Big Horn Mountains of southeastern Montana.

Lone traders and trappers wandered into Montana after that, but more than sixty years passed before another expedition was launched. Through the Louisiana Purchase of 1803, President Thomas Jefferson bought the Louisiana region from France. This vast, sprawling expanse of land extended west from the Mississippi River and included most of present-day Montana. But even at the time of its sale, no one was sure where Louisiana's western boundaries lay. To find out more about the region, Jefferson appointed Meriwether Lewis and William Clark to lead an expedition that would travel all the way to the Pacific Ocean.

THE LEWIS AND CLARK EXPEDITION

Lewis and Clark made the first systematic exploration of Montana's terrain. Their well-kept journals reveal in beautiful detail the geography and native cultures they encountered. Setting out from St. Louis, Missouri, in May 1804, the two explorers headed up the Missouri River with a party of thirty-two men.

While passing through North Dakota, Lewis and Clark added several more people to their expedition. One was a guide named Sacagawea ("Bird Woman"), a Shoshone woman who knew the wilderness trails and passes. Another was her husband, Toussaint Charbonneau, a French-Canadian who, according to Lewis, "cannot swim and is perhaps the most timid waterman in the world."

In April 1805, the party arrived at the mouth of the Yellowstone River, on the eastern border of present-day Montana. Continuing up the Missouri, they gave names to many of the geographical features they encountered—the Marias River, the Great Falls of the Missouri, Gates of the Mountains canyon, the Prickly Pear Valley, and many others.

Perhaps Lewis felt he had to justify naming the Marias River after his cousin Maria. "The hue of the waters of this turbulent and troubled stream," he wrote, "but illy comport with the pure celestial virtues and amiable qualifications of that lovely fair one; but on the other hand it is a noble river." No noble feelings moved Lewis to name the Prickly Pear Valley, however. When he

A nineteenth-century depiction of Lewis and Clark at the Great Falls of the Missouri

first trekked into the valley, he got seventeen prickly pear cactus thorns in his feet.

At last the expedition arrived at the spot they named Three Forks. There they discovered that the source of the Missouri River was not a lake or a spring, like the sources of most rivers. Instead, the Missouri rose at the juncture of three other streams, which they named the Jefferson, Gallatin, and Madison rivers.

Lewis and Clark continued west through the present-day states of Idaho, Oregon, and Washington. Following the Columbia River to the Pacific Ocean, they completed their quest for a Northwest Passage. On their return trip in 1806, they again passed through Montana. This time the expedition split into two parties. Lewis explored the Marias River in the north and Clark followed the Yellowstone in the south. They reunited on the Missouri and headed for home, having explored more of Montana than any white person ever had before.

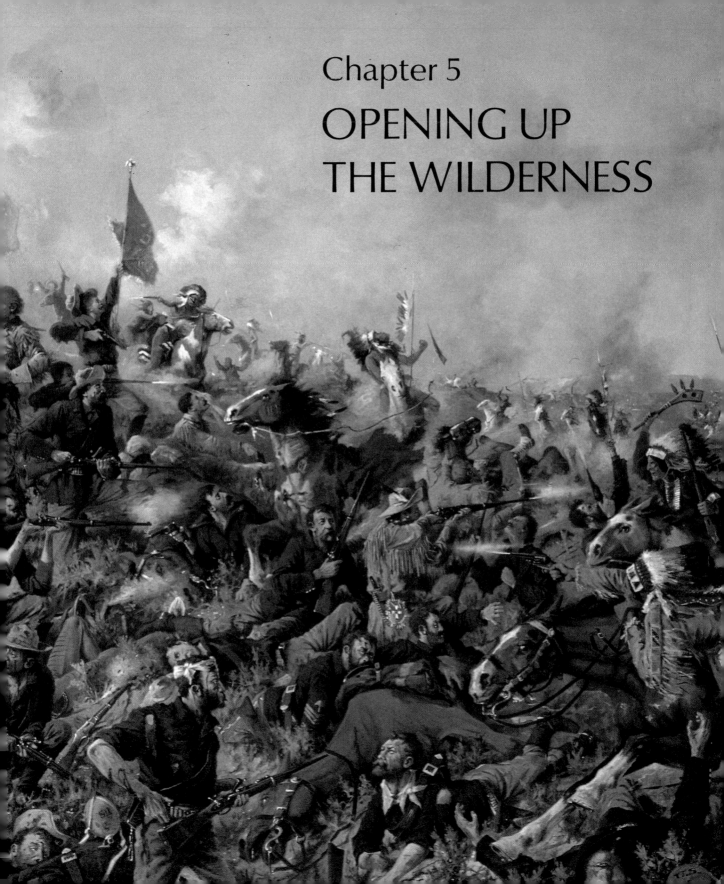

Chapter 5
OPENING UP
THE WILDERNESS

OPENING UP THE WILDERNESS

TRADERS AND TRADING POSTS

Even before Lewis and Clark embarked on their expedition, trappers and "mountain men" were penetrating Montana to hunt fur-bearing animals and to trade with the Indians. The explorers had run into nearly a dozen of these men. Many of them were independent, while others worked for trading companies. The British-owned Hudson's Bay Company and North West Company, as well as French-Canadian, Spanish, and American traders, were viciously competing for the rich trapping grounds of the American Northwest.

When Lewis and Clark returned to St. Louis, traders were thrilled with the reports of their explorations. One trader, a Spaniard named Manuel Lisa, hastily gathered partners together and formed the Missouri Fur Company. They embarked on a trading expedition up the Yellowstone River and, in 1807, set up Montana's first trading post at the mouth of the Bighorn River. Lisa sent out one of his men, John Colter, to arrange trade deals with the Indians. Colter's treacherous wintertime journey through the present-day Yellowstone Park region gave the area the name "Colter's Hell."

While Lewis and Clark were heading up the Missouri, a Canadian named David Thompson, working for the North West Company, had been exploring the Northwest. After mapping the Columbia River region, Thompson crossed the Rocky Mountains

Fur trappers (left), including such "mountain men" as Jim Bridger (right), began penetrating the Montana region in the early 1800s.

into what is now Montana. In 1808, he established Kootenai House, a trading post on the Kootenai River. A year later, he established Salish House on the Clark Fork River near present-day Thompson Falls.

One after another, more trading companies were forming. Millionaire John Jacob Astor founded the Pacific Fur Company and later the American Fur Company, intending to spread a trading empire across the Northwest. Astor and others welcomed the Convention of 1818, an agreement between Britain and the United States. In it, Britain recognized the 49th parallel as America's northern border east of the Rockies. This meant that Canadians and other foreigners were barred from trading or trapping south of that line.

In 1822, William Ashley formed the Rocky Mountain Fur Company, which employed famed mountain men Jim Bridger and

Fort Union in 1866

Jedediah Smith. These enterprising adventurers were among
Montana's most colorful characters. Bridger was once wounded in
the back by an arrowhead that stuck there for three years. Asked
if the wound ever got infected, Bridger replied, "In the mountains,
meat never spoils."

Pierre Chouteau, Kenneth McKenzie, and other St. Louis men
became powerful fur traders in the Missouri River Valley.
Forming a branch of the American Fur Company, they established
the Fort Union trading post on Montana's present eastern border
in 1828. The company continued up the Missouri River to
establish Fort Benton, an important trade and navigation center.
Established in 1847, Fort Benton is Montana's oldest permanent
white settlement.

Meanwhile, the American government continued to negotiate
with the British over land ownership and trade rights in the
Northwest. In the Oregon Treaty of 1846, the United States and

Great Britain agreed that northwest Montana would become American territory.

BIG IGNACE AND THE BLACK ROBES

> When I tell my poor blind people . . . that I did not bring the book, no word will be spoken by our old men or by our young braves. One by one they will rise and go out in silence. My people will die in darkness . . . .
> —Attributed to an anonymous Indian in 1831, requesting a missionary for the Salish

Big Ignace was a Canadian Iroquois who had converted to Christianity. After working as a trapper and oarsman for the North West Company, he came to live among the Salish Indians in Montana's Rockies. Big Ignace enthralled the Salish with tales of the "Black Robes" (Catholic priests) and of their "Book of Heaven." The Salish soon wished for a Black Robe of their own. In four separate trips—1831, 1835, 1837, and 1839—Salish delegations journeyed down the Missouri River to St. Louis to ask for a missionary. Big Ignace led two of the expeditions, but completed only one. Sioux attackers killed him and the rest of the delegates on the 1837 trip.

Protestant ministers would not satisfy the Salish; they had to have a Black Robe. Finally, Bishop Rosati assigned Pierre-Jean De Smet, a young Belgian priest of the Jesuit order, to the Salish mission.

De Smet arrived among the Salish in 1840, left, and returned the next year with six more missionaries. Settling in the Bitterroot Valley, they established St. Mary's Mission and began teaching the Salish to read and write. In the spring of 1842, De Smet sowed oats, wheat, and potatoes at St. Mary's Mission, and the Salish

harvested their first crops in the fall. In 1854, Father Adrian
Hoecken built St. Ignatius Mission near Flathead Lake.

SURVEY TEAMS AND CATTLE DRIVES

After gold was discovered in California in 1848, thousands of
fortune hunters joined the westward rush for California's gold.
Both the federal government and private railroad companies saw
the need to lay tracks across the West. Railroad men envisioned a
transcontinental railroad system that stretched from the Atlantic
Ocean on the east to the Pacific Ocean on the west.

Teams of army surveyors began to arrive in Montana to find
suitable railroad routes across the territory. General Isaac Stevens
surveyed a possible route across northern Montana in 1853.
Lieutenant John Mullan built a wagon road from the Columbia
River to Fort Benton between 1859 and 1863.

In 1866, rancher Nelson Story drove a herd of one thousand
Texas longhorn cattle from Texas to graze on Montana's grassy
plains. Thus began eastern Montana's cattle business, soon to
become one of Montana's major industries.

Railroads and ranching came to serve each other well. It was
not long before railroad cars rumbled across Montana, taking
fattened cattle to markets.

MONTANA'S GOLD RUSH

Montana's Indians had long known of gold in the territory, but
it meant nothing to them. In the 1840s, Father De Smet knew
there was gold in the western mountains, too. He kept quiet about
the gold, however, hoping to protect the Indians and their land
from being overrun.

St. Ignatius Mission, near Flathead Lake, was founded in 1854.

In 1857, two brothers, James and Granville Stuart, found traces of gold near Gold Creek in the Deer Lodge Valley, in southwestern Montana. Rumor had it that a prospector named François Finlay had found gold in the same area the year before. The Stuarts returned in 1862 and began mining in earnest. As word got around, prospectors began trickling in.

The big rush for Montana's gold, however, began in 1862, when John White struck rich deposits on Grasshopper Creek. Overnight, the town of Bannack rose from the Beaverhead Valley.

Montana's most fabulous gold discovery of all came in 1863 in Alder Gulch, about 75 miles (121 kilometers) from Bannack. Gold rushers flooded the gulch, founding Virginia City and Nevada City. According to one newspaperman, "thousands of tenderfeet were wildly filing claims." In one year, Alder Gulch yielded $10 million worth of gold.

Bannack Sheriff Henry Plummer and his gang conducted dozens of bloody stagecoach robberies in the 1860s.

Another group of prospectors, meanwhile, had been panning for gold in the western hills—with no luck. In July 1864, as they gazed down upon a gulch in the Prickly Pear Valley, one of them said, "Well, boys, that little gulch in the Prickly Pear is our last chance." They struck it big at that spot—and named it "Last Chance Gulch."

Within weeks, a booming mining town appeared. In October 1864, the miners of Last Chance Gulch met to draw up rules and regulations and to choose a better-sounding name. They settled on "Helena," the name of the hometown of a miner from Minnesota.

In the same area, Confederate Gulch, Grizzly Gulch, and Rattlesnake Gulch yielded rich gold finds. With each strike, mining camps became boomtowns. Chinese immigrants and a few newly freed southern blacks came to Montana, becoming the territory's underclasses. Lawlessness prevailed in the wild young towns. Many miners got rich quick and spent their entire fortunes in saloons, dance halls, and gambling parlors. Disputes were occasionally settled by the fastest gun.

ROAD AGENTS AND VIGILANTES

All this gold in a land with virtually no law enforcement created an outlaw's paradise. In the 1860s, traveling bandits known as road agents preyed on miners, robbing and killing them on the road. The 75-mile (121-kilometer) stretch between Bannack and Virginia City was especially dangerous. There the law was surely no help, for Bannack Sheriff Henry Plummer himself led a notorious gang of bandits along that road. Using secret codes and chalk marks on stagecoaches, Plummer's road agents robbed and killed dozens of people.

When the citizens of Bannack and Virginia City uncovered Plummer's operation, they organized a "vigilance committee" to snuff it out. These vigilantes, as they were called, rounded up the bandits and executed them, often by hanging them on the spot. In January 1864, they nabbed Plummer himself and hanged him.

MONTANA TERRITORY

By the mid-1860s, with its growing population, Montana clearly required an organized government. In 1863, Congress created Idaho Territory, which included present-day Montana. But the Idaho government, seated west of the Rockies, had trouble controlling affairs in the mountains and beyond. To help the region govern itself more efficiently, Congress separated the eastern part of Idaho Territory and declared it Montana Territory on May 26, 1864.

Montana's first territorial legislature convened in Bannack in 1864. The following year, Montana's territorial legislators voted to move the capital to Virginia City.

CUSTER'S LAST STAND

As wave after wave of settlers moved into Montana, they claimed land on which the Indians had lived and hunted for centuries. First, whites arrived to hunt and trap fur-bearing animals. Later they hunted buffalo, an important source of food, clothing, shelter, and tools for the Indians. Farmers staked valley-bottom claims and cleared fields, while ranchers fenced off water sources as they spread out across the fertile plains. Prospectors and miners swarmed in by the thousands.

Many Indians simply retreated to more remote areas. Others, such as the Sioux, attacked settlers. United States Army troops were sent to Montana to protect the settlers and fight off the Indians.

Montana's Indian conflicts came to a head in June 1876, in the Battle of the Little Bighorn, also known as Custer's Last Stand. As Lieutenant Colonel George Armstrong Custer led his cavalry regiment into the valley of the Little Bighorn River, he spotted an encampment of thousands of Sioux, Cheyenne, and other Plains Indians. Custer split his men into three groups, perhaps hoping to surround the Indians. Major Marcus Reno, with about 130 men, fought a desperate, two-day battle, suffering heavy casualties. On June 25, Custer, with only about 225 cavalrymen, marched to the Little Bighorn. No one knows why Custer rode forth to fight a battle in which his men were hopelessly outnumbered. Perhaps his past successes as an Indian fighter had gone to his head. It took less than an hour for the thousands of

Lt. Col. George Custer (left) was killed in the Battle of the Little Bighorn, shown here (above) from an Indian's perspective.

Indian warriors to decimate Custer's troops. All the Americans engaged in this bloody battle, including Custer, were killed. No one knows how many Indian casualties there were.

"I WILL FIGHT NO MORE FOREVER"

In 1877, United States Army troops were directed to move eight hundred Nez Perce Indians from their traditional homeland in Oregon to a reservation in Idaho. Under Chief Joseph, the Nez Perce escaped their army escorts and embarked on a five-month dash toward safety in Canada. The army followed in hot pursuit, engaging the Indians in a two-day battle at the Big Hole, a few days' travel into Montana.

Their numbers cut down, the Nez Perce continued on through Montana. Colonel Nelson A. Miles caught up with the exhausted Indians in the Bears Paw Mountains, only about 30 miles (48 kilometers) south of the Canada border. On October 5, 1877, after a three-day battle, Chief Joseph surrendered. The Nez Perce who were still alive were sent to Indian Territory (present-day Oklahoma). Finally, in 1885, the remaining two hundred were sent back to Idaho and Washington State.

Before he surrendered, Chief Joseph made this speech to his warriors: "I am tired of fighting. Our chiefs are killed. . . . It is cold and we have no blankets. The little children are freezing to death. . . . I want to have time to look for my children and see how many of them I can find. Maybe I shall find them among the dead. Hear me, my chiefs. I am tired. My heart is sick and sad. From where the sun now stands I will fight no more forever."

THE RICHEST HILL ON EARTH

Beginning in the 1860s, the hills around Butte were to play a major part in Montana's history for over a century. Butte's first gold deposits turned up in 1864, and silver was discovered there in 1875. William A. Clark opened Butte's Travonia silver mine, and for the next decade, Butte was Montana's "Silver City."

Meanwhile, an Irishman named Marcus Daly, mining for silver in Butte, struck one of the richest copper veins in the world. His copper mine in Butte, opened in 1881, transformed the little town into a big city. Daly also founded the town of Anaconda, northwest of Butte, where he erected the great Washoe Smelter. William Clark joined the copper rush, adding copper mines to his other holdings.

So much copper came out of Butte Hill that it was called the "Richest Hill on Earth." Butte became the center of Montana's industrial life. Miners from England, Ireland, Wales, and other countries rushed in to work the mines. By the 1890s, copper had become Montana's most important mineral.

In 1877, while attempting to lead his people to safety in Canada, Nez Perce Chief Joseph (left) was forced to surrender to United States troops in the Bears Paw Mountains just south of the Canada border.

THE WAR OF THE COPPER KINGS

Marcus Daly and William Clark soon came to be known as the "copper kings." Both became fabulously wealthy and powerful, and their bitter competition spilled over into politics. Daly tried to make his smelter town of Anaconda the capital. Clark pushed the legislators to vote for Helena, which won by a narrow margin. Each of them, attempting to sway public opinion in his own direction, owned an important Montana newspaper; Daly controlled the respected Anaconda *Standard,* and Clark owned the Butte *Miner.*

When Clark tried to win a United States Senate seat in 1899, Daly decided to do everything in his power to stop him. Clark won anyway, but resigned when a Senate committee—spurred on by reports in the *Standard* that Clark had engaged in bribery—

Underground copper miners at work in a Butte mine around 1910

began to investigate him. He won the seat again in 1901 with the help of Frederick Augustus Heinze, another copper magnate.

The mining operations of both Daly and Clark were eventually absorbed into the Anaconda Copper Mining Company, a giant corporation founded by Daly. Well into the twentieth century, "The Company," as it was called, was a powerful force in the state. It owned Montana's major electric power utilities and controlled many of the state's influential banks and newspapers. Most of the profits from these enterprises ended up out of state. According to author John Gunther, Montana became the "nearest to a 'colony' of any American state."

GROWTH AND STATEHOOD

In the 1880s, Montana's population nearly quadrupled, growing from 39,159 to 142,924. Mining accounted for much of this

Cowboys branding calves on a Miles City ranch in the 1890s

growth, but ranching was thriving as well. In cities and towns, new businesses were bustling to serve the needs of miners, farmers, and ranchers. The Northern Pacific Railroad, completed through Montana in 1883, boosted the cattle industry. Ranchers were finally able to ship their cattle to markets in the Midwest and on the East Coast. Farmers welcomed the railroads, too, as a way to ship their produce to new markets.

Montanans, who had first appealed to Congress for statehood in 1866, made another appeal in 1884. Finally, in 1889, Congress passed a Montana enabling act. This allowed the territory to draw up a proposed state constitution. Delegates met in a constitutional convention and composed a constitution. After Montana voters ratified it, it was sent on to Washington, D.C., where Congress gave its approval. On November 8, 1889, Montana joined the Union as the forty-first state. Joseph K. Toole was elected Montana's first governor.

Chapter 6
THE TWENTIETH CENTURY

THE TWENTIETH CENTURY

As Montana entered the twentieth century, it embarked on an era of change. New dams harnessed its rivers and new food-processing industries expanded its economy. Congress established Glacier National Park in 1910, and tourism became a growing trade.

In 1916, Montana voters elected Jeannette Rankin to the United States House of Representatives. An ardent pacifist and social activist, Rankin was the first woman to serve in Congress. She was the only member to vote against the United States' entry into both World War I and World War II. Together, she and her fellow Montanans were to witness many bitter and turbulent years.

MINERS, UNIONS, AND STRIKES

> Fixed up miner with scalp wound. Ditto with crushed finger. . . . Admitted miner with bruised head. . . . Was confronted with a miner with crushed foot. . . . Sewed up [a miner's] head with a vim of determination. Dismissed him into the mysterious air of night. . . . Four miners decided to get hurt for a change. Fixed them all up & sent them on their way rejoicing. . . .
> —From *Diary of a Night Nurse,* by Beatrice Murphy

Beatrice Murphy's diary is spiked with jokes, some gentle and some grim. She needed a sense of humor as she ministered to

Jeannette Rankin was the first woman to serve in Congress.

victims of Butte's mining accidents. Almost every night, she was faced with crushed feet and fingers or wounded heads.

Butte's miners, however, had no sense of humor about their jobs. They wanted safer working conditions, compensation for job-related injuries, and higher wages. Miners' labor unions, started in the 1870s, had grown to be very powerful by the early 1900s. With that power came violence, corruption, and union leaders' feuds. Butte was put under martial law in 1914, and its mines were declared nonunion, or "open shop."

In the following years, workers in other industries maintained trade unions, but labor relations were still strained. A radical labor organization called the Industrial Workers of the World (IWW) agitated union members and encouraged strikes. Butte's mines reverted to "closed shop" in 1934 after miners' and other tradesmen's unions were reorganized.

National Guardsmen were sent in to keep the peace when Butte miners agitated for better working conditions in 1914.

FARMERS' WOES

In the early 1900s, thousands of farmers arrived in Montana to farm the eastern plains. They swarmed in from all over the country, as well as from Germany and Scandinavia. One million acres (0.4 million hectares) of land claims had been filed by 1909 and 5 million acres (2 million hectares) by 1910. By 1922, the claims had reached 93 million acres (38 million hectares).

Most of Montana's farmers planted their acreage in flax, oats, and wheat. As shelter against the bitterly cold winters, many built ramshackle wooden shacks. A few, however, lived in sod houses built partly underground.

During World War I (1914-18), Montana's farmers were able to get good prices for their wheat, but the bounty did not last. Beginning in 1917, a gradually worsening drought crept across

Montana's farmland. By 1919, brittle stalks of parched crops lay in the relentless sun from the Rocky Mountains to the Dakota line. Thousands of people went broke, then homeless. Sad little armies of defeated farmers left the state in droves, hoping to mend their broken lives in greener pastures.

High winds swept across the barren plains in 1920, carrying the topsoil away. Frightening swarms of grasshoppers ate whatever grass and grain remained. As periods of drought and rain alternated over the next decade, Montana's farmers learned to work with the extremes. With drought-resistant wheat, crop diversification, strip farming, and mechanized farm equipment, farmers eventually stood a chance of drawing a profit from the soil.

The weather was not the farmers' only complaint. They felt they were paying more than their fair share of taxes, while the state's mines were getting away too easily. Under progressive governor Joseph M. Dixon, who served from 1921 to 1925, the state legislature passed a tax on mineral extraction.

THE DEPRESSION ERA

No sooner was Montana's farming revival underway than the Great Depression hit the nation in 1929. Demand for Montana's minerals and lumber dropped as manufacturing activity slowed. Prices for farm products dropped, too. Mines closed, businesses folded, and farms failed. One-fourth of Montanans were collecting federal relief money by 1935.

Under President Franklin D. Roosevelt's New Deal programs, millions of dollars' worth of federal assistance poured into Montana. Many federal construction projects helped keep people employed. Construction of Fort Peck Dam on the Missouri River

Federal work-relief projects, such as the building of roads (left) and the construction of Fort Peck Dam (right), provided jobs for Montanans during the Great Depression.

was completed in 1940, providing irrigation, hydroelectric power, and recreation opportunities. Roads were built, water reclamation projects were started, and electric power lines were extended to rural areas.

WORLD WAR II AND THE POSTWAR BOOM

World War II, which the United States entered in 1941, lifted the state out of its economic miseries. Wartime demand for food and metals revived Montana's farms and mines. Montana's wheat and beef were used for rations and its copper was needed for munitions and aircraft.

As businesses revived after the war, people moved from rural areas to cities for jobs. In the 1950s, for the first time, the state's city dwellers grew to outnumber those in rural areas.

Helena's main street in the 1930s

At the same time, Montana's energy industry took a new turn. Oil was discovered in the Williston Basin of eastern Montana and western North Dakota, and wells began operating in 1951. Aluminum joined the ranks of Montana's marketable minerals. The Anaconda Company expanded to include the Anaconda Aluminum Company and built a large aluminum plant in 1955.

New dams built in the 1960s provided irrigation and hydroelectric power. The dams also created lakes for boating, waterskiing, and fishing. Record numbers of tourists poured into Montana's national and state parks, recreation areas, resorts, dude ranches, and ski areas.

GRIM YEARS

A nationwide fuel shortage in the 1970s increased the demand for Montana's petroleum and natural-gas resources. Utility and

Butte's open-pit copper mine was closed in 1983.

energy companies also began large-scale strip mining of coal in the southeastern part of the state.

For Montana's farmers and environmentalists, the strip-mined landscape was the last straw. In 1973, the state legislature passed the Montana Strip Mine Reclamation Act and the Utility Siting Act. In 1975, the severance tax on nonferrous coal extraction was raised to 30 percent. Half the revenues from this tax were set aside to revitalize areas ravaged by mining and to build roads, schools, and other public facilities in those areas.

The 1980s dealt Montana one devastating blow after another. Low worldwide copper prices forced Anaconda's copper smelter to shut down in 1980. Butte's open-pit copper mine, the last of Anaconda's once-vast holdings, was closed in 1983. Thousands of workers lost their jobs. A sharp drop in worldwide oil prices in the 1980s hurt Montana's petroleum industry. In the mid-1980s, another drought took its toll on the state's farms. Montana's population, after peaking at 826,000 in 1985, shrank to 799,065 by 1990.

Montana's beauty continues to lure thousands of tourists to Big Sky Country each year.

RUSH TO THE BIG SKY

The land of the Big Sky continues to attract tourists. Exiles from hectic, big-city life are moving to Montana to start simpler lives close to the land. Some succeed at ranching or farming, though many come unprepared for Montana's harsh winters. The 1980s saw an influx of well-known writers, entertainers, and business moguls to Montana's resorts and wilderness areas.

While the newcomers help boost the taxable population, many natives fear that their state will be overrun by outsiders who are out of touch with Montana's soul. Remembering history, some fear that newcomers may exploit the state's natural resources or upset the balance of nature under the Big Sky.

As Montanans look toward the twenty-first century, they hope to find new ways to benefit from their natural resources. They know these assets are their greatest wealth and their last, best hope for the future.

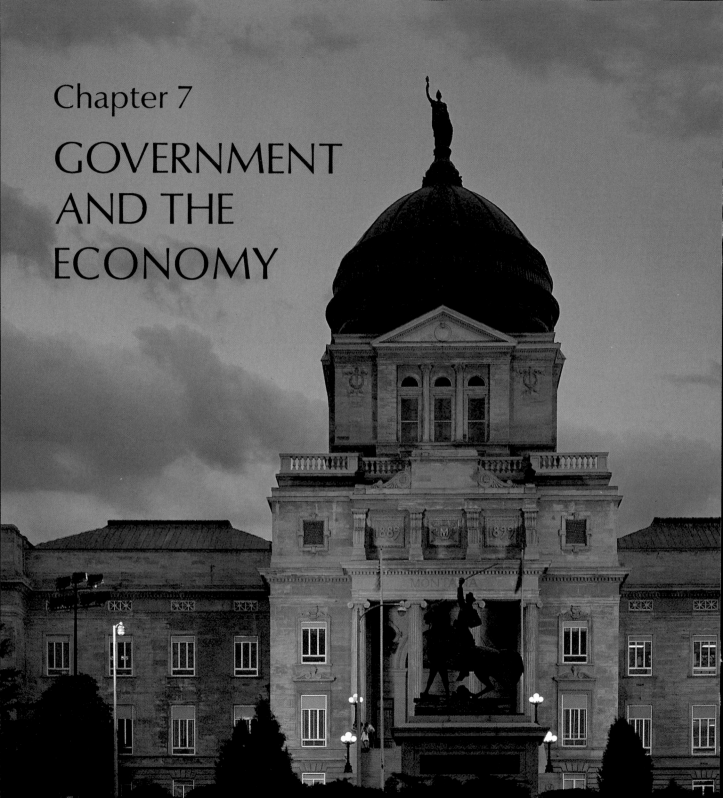

Chapter 7
GOVERNMENT AND THE ECONOMY

GOVERNMENT AND THE ECONOMY

Montana's first state constitution, enacted upon statehood in 1889, was the law of the land for eighty-four years. In 1972, a state constitutional convention drew up a new constitution, which went into effect in 1973. The new constitution provided, among other things, that voters decide every twenty years whether to call a constitutional convention, that eighteen-year-olds have adults' rights, that city and county governments be reorganized as needed, and that presidential primaries be held.

GOVERNMENT

Like the federal government, Montana's state government consists of three branches. The legislative branch, or state legislature, makes state laws; the executive branch, or office of the governor, carries out the laws; and the judicial branch, or state court system, interprets the laws.

Montana's state legislature, like the United States Congress, consists of a senate and a house of representatives. Voters in Montana's senatorial districts elect fifty state senators to serve four-year terms. So that the business of lawmaking flows smoothly, half the senators come up for election every two years. One state representative is elected from each of Montana's one hundred representative districts. State representatives serve two-year terms.

Regular sessions of the legislature begin in Helena on the first Monday in January of odd-numbered years. Legislators remain in session for up to ninety workdays. They or the governor may also call special sessions if the need arises. If the governor vetoes a bill that the legislators have passed, they may override the veto by a two-thirds vote in both houses.

Montana's governor heads the executive branch of state government. The governor serves a four-year term and may be reelected any number of times. Voters also elect a number of other executive officers to four-year terms, including the lieutenant governor, secretary of state, attorney general, superintendent of public instruction, state auditor, and public service commissioners. Heads of seventeen executive departments and directors of several state institutions are appointed by the governor.

The state supreme court is Montana's highest court. Voters elect its chief justice and six associate justices for eight-year terms. Judges in Montana's twenty district courts, elected for six-year terms, try major civil and criminal cases. Each of Montana's fifty-six counties elects at least one justice of the peace to preside over a justice court. Many towns also have municipal and police courts.

In most Montana counties, voters elect three commissioners to administer county business. Cities and towns are governed either by a mayor and city council or by a city council and city manager.

EDUCATION

Compared to the nation as a whole, Montanans are more literate and better educated. Montana's literacy rate is 92 percent, while only 87 percent of the nation's people can read and write. About 75 percent of Montana adults are high-school graduates, while the national average is 67 percent. Eighteen percent of the state's adults also have college degrees.

Montana's first schools were opened in 1863 for children in the

The rotunda of the Montana State Capitol in Helena

Bannack and Nevada City mining camps. The new state's legislature formed a state board of education in 1893 and provided for free county schools in 1897. Today, Montana's Board of Public Education supervises the public school system.

By law, children in Montana are required to attend school from age eight to age sixteen. In the late 1980s, about 152,200 students were enrolled in Montana's 774 public elementary and secondary schools. Schools that have a high percentage of Native American students must provide classes in Native American culture. The state also maintains such special services as transportation, occupational and physical therapy, and home-bound programs for disabled students. More than one hundred private schools operate in the state.

For higher education, Montana students can choose among the state's six public colleges and universities, three private colleges,

The University of Montana, in Missoula, was founded in 1893.

three public community colleges, and seven tribally controlled community colleges. The state institutions are Montana State University, in Bozeman; the University of Montana, in Missoula; Eastern Montana College, in Billings; Western Montana College, in Dillon; Northern Montana College, in Havre; and the College of Mineral Science and Technology, in Butte. The Roman Catholic church operates Carroll College, in Helena; and the College of Great Falls, in Great Falls. Together, the Congregational, Methodist, and Presbyterian churches run Rocky Mountain College in Billings. In addition, there are vocational-technical training centers in Billings, Butte, Great Falls, Helena, and Missoula.

STATE FINANCE AND EMPLOYMENT

Montana draws its state revenues, or income, from a number of sources. The federal government provides about one-third of the state's revenues. Over half the remaining revenues come from income, mineral-extraction, real-estate, livestock, and business taxes. Montana is one of only five states in the nation that does not levy a state sales tax. Severance taxes for coal extraction and property taxes for local mineral proceeds are a great benefit to the whole state. One-half of these natural-resource revenues go to Montana's Resource Indemnity Trust Fund, set up to clean up the environment and provide for the future.

About 30 percent of Montana's yearly state expenditures support health and social services. Another 25 percent goes toward education and cultural programs. Transportation, especially the state highway system, receives about 18 percent of Montana's total expenditures. Other state funds develop recreational areas and keep the state government running.

Government is Montana's largest single employer. Federal, state, and local government activities employ about 26 percent of the labor force. Government industries include military bases, national and state parklands, and public schools. About 53 percent of Montana's workers are involved in various nongovernment service industries, such as wholesale and retail trade, medical and health services, finance, insurance, and real estate. While manufacturing occupies 22 percent of the nation's workers, it employs only 7 percent of Montana's labor force. Nine percent of Montana's laborers work in farming occupations, compared to the national average of 3 percent.

MINING

It could easily be said that mining created Montana. Gold, silver, and copper rushes built a population and an economic base that has continued to grow over the years. Today, petroleum is

Oil, produced in eastern and central Montana, is the state's leading mineral product.

Montana's most important mineral, accounting for about half the state's mining income. Oil wells in the Powder River and Williston basins are the largest producers. Natural gas is found in the northern part of the state.

Coal is next in importance. Montana has the largest coal reserves in the United States. Large-scale open-pit strip mining for coal dominates the Colstrip region of southeastern Montana. Since strip mining ravages the landscape, laws have been passed requiring coal-mining companies to restore the environment. A nationwide energy shortage in the 1970s was a tremendous boost for Montana's oil, gas, and coal industries.

Hidden in the western mountains are deposits of copper, gold, lead, silver, and zinc. Montana is still one of the nation's leading gold, silver, and copper producers. The late 1980s saw a rebirth in the state's gold and silver operations. No other state produces

Most of Montana's commercial timber is sent to sawmills to be cut into lumber.

more talc, vermiculite, and sapphires. Montana's other important mining products include aluminum, gemstones, phosphate, limestone, gypsum, chromite, barite, clay, sand, and gravel.

A sharp drop in oil prices in the mid-1980s struck a devastating blow to Montana's energy industries. The Anaconda Company's withdrawal from copper mining also caused an economic decline. As national and worldwide energy prices increase, however, Montana's oil, gas, and coal industries are growing. Several new metals mines are opening in the state, too.

MANUFACTURING

Lumber and wood products are Montana's most important manufactured goods, although the lumber market declined somewhat in the 1980s. Most of the state's commercial timber is made into boards. After loggers fell the trees, sawmills cut the logs into boards for construction. Other wood is made into paper, pulpwood, or plywood. Missoula has both a paper mill and a plywood plant. Plywood is also manufactured in Columbia Falls and Libby.

Processed food is next in importance among Montana's manufactured goods. Sugar beets are processed into sugar at refineries in Billings and Sidney, and wheat is milled into flour in Billings and Great Falls. Processing plants around the state prepare and package cattle feed, dairy products, meat, and vegetables. The state's other manufacturing activities include mineral processing and oil refining.

AGRICULTURE AND FORESTRY

Drought and insect infestation are constant threats to Montana's farms. Nevertheless, agriculture is the major source of income in eastern Montana. There are about twenty-five thousand farms in Montana. Most of the farmland is used for grazing cattle, and livestock provides about two-fifths of Montana's farm income. Beef, dairy products, eggs, pigs and hogs, sheep, wool, and honey are the major livestock products.

Montana's farmers plant various crops on about one-fourth of the state's farmland. Wheat, accounting for one-fourth of the state's farm income, is the leading crop. Montana is one of the nation's leading wheat producers. The state also exports large quantities of wheat to Pacific Rim nations. Other valuable crops are barley, sugar beets, hay, flax, potatoes, and mustard seed.

In western Montana, lumbering is a major source of income. Forests cover about one-fourth of Montana's land area. Montana is one of the leading softwood producers in the country. The

Although irrigation (left) helps a variety of crops to grow in Montana, most of the state's farmland is used for grazing cattle (right).

Douglas fir is the state's most important commercial tree, followed by cedar, pine, larch, and spruce. State economists are concerned that the depressed national lumber market, coupled with timber shortages in western Montana, may hurt lumbering operations in the future.

TRANSPORTATION

Throughout Montana's history, transportation has been vital to its economy. People and goods have had to travel great distances to reach markets and other destinations. Montana's rail system has come a long way since the Utah & Northern Railroad first opened in Montana Territory in 1880. Today, the state's freight

Passenger trains serve about ten Montana cities.

and passenger trains run on about 3,480 miles (5,600 kilometers) of track.

About three-fifths of Montana's 71,000 miles (114,260 kilometers) of roadways are paved. The state highway system maintains excellent roads throughout the state. In addition, several interstate highways serve Montana. Interstate 90 joins Interstate 94 at Billings, providing an east-west passage across the whole state. Missoula, Butte, Bozeman, Livingston, Billings, Miles City, and Glendive all lie along this route. Interstate 15 is the major north-south highway in the western part of the state. Between the southwestern corner and the Canada border, it passes through Butte, Helena, and Great Falls.

Montana joined the aerospace age in 1928, when National Parks Airways began flying between Great Falls and Salt Lake City,

Utah. Today, there are about 170 airports throughout the state. The airports at Billings, Bozeman, and Great Falls are the state's major commercial air facilities. Some of Montana's large farms have their own private airfields.

COMMUNICATION

Montana's first newspaper was the *Montana Post*, started in Virginia City in 1864. After hauling their printing press up the Missouri by steamboat, its founders printed the paper in a cabin cellar and sold it for fifty cents a copy—payment in gold dust acceptable. In the following years, weekly papers sprang up in many of Montana's gold-mining towns.

In the 1890s, copper kings William Clark and Marcus Daly gained control of most of Montana's important newspapers, each wanting to make sure that his mining operations were shown in a favorable light. This state of affairs came to be called Montana's "captive press." A couple of newspapers managed to remain independent, notably the *Great Falls Tribune*. Another was the Billings *Vociferator*, whose slogan was "We did not come to Montana for our health."

Today, about eighty newspapers are published in Montana, eleven of them daily papers. The *Billings Gazette*, the *Great Falls Tribune*, and the *Missoulian* have the largest circulations.

Montana's first radio station was KFBB, which began broadcasting in Great Falls in 1922. Its first television stations were KXLF and KOPR, both of which began operation in Butte in 1953. Today, about fifteen television stations and ninety-five radio stations broadcast in Montana. In recent years, cable television has become so popular in Montana that some have called the satellite dish Montana's "new official state flower."

Chapter 8
ARTS AND LEISURE

ARTS AND LEISURE

Though geographically distant from the nation's cultural centers, Montanans are very much in touch with both their artistic heritage and their own creativity. A lively interest in the arts flourishes at the grass-roots level, from fiddlers' ensembles to experimental theater to local art fairs and regional arts councils.

The state government encourages the arts, too. The Montana Arts Council, a state agency, sponsors arts programs in the schools and awards grants for artists and writers. Other arts organizations include the Montana Performing Arts Consortium, a nonprofit coalition of performers and presenters; the Montana Institute of the Arts, based in Bozeman; and the Montana Cultural Advocacy, a pro-arts activist organization.

FINE ART

Montana's most renowned and beloved artist is painter and sculptor Charles M. Russell. His dramatic and sensitive portrayals of the history and culture of the West represent a major contribution to American art. Born in St. Louis, Russell arrived in Montana at the age of sixteen, and worked as a cowboy on ranches in the Judith Basin and Great Falls regions. He produced much of his work in his log-cabin studio in Great Falls. Russell, who died in 1926, also wrote and illustrated the books *Trails Plowed Under* and *Good Medicine*. His studio, home, and an extensive collection of his works are included in the C. M. Russell Museum complex in Great Falls.

Charles M. Russell's *Lewis and Clark Meeting Indians at Ross' Hole*

Collections of Russell's work also appear in the state capitol, at the Montana Historical Society, and in many institutions and galleries throughout the state. His painting *Lewis and Clark Meeting Indians at Ross' Hole*, considered by many to be his masterpiece, hangs above the rostrum in the Montana State Capitol's house of representatives.

Also in the capitol are paintings by another Montana artist, Edgar Paxson. After having lived in several Montana towns, Paxson built a studio in Missoula. He worked on his masterpiece, *Custer's Last Stand*, for twenty-one years. Now at the University of Montana, it portrays more than two hundred Indians and soldiers.

Ralph DeCamp was another of Montana's noted artists. Known for his landscapes, DeCamp lived and worked in Helena from 1896 to 1924. Several of his paintings, including his best-known work, *Gates of the Mountains*, hang in the state capitol.

Will James of Pryor was a self-taught Western artist and a great admirer of Charles Russell. Also a Western novelist, James illustrated his books with action-packed drawings of cowboy life.

PERFORMING ARTS

Montana audiences enjoy music, theater, and dance events throughout the state. The Billings Symphony Orchestra and Chorale offers an annual season of symphonic and choral music, as well as an annual pops concert. Bozeman, Missoula, and Helena also support symphony orchestras. In the summertime, local audiences enjoy presentations by Helena's municipal band and Great Falls's Symphony Association.

Classical and contemporary string quartet works are the specialty of the Cascade Quartet of Great Falls. The Yellowstone Chamber Players offer a concert series in Billings and also tour the state. Young fiddlers in the Dillon Junior Fiddlers Association present concerts and musical revues. Several towns offer community concert series, and the University of Montana and Montana State University present concerts and recitals.

Theater ensembles in the state include the Actors Theatre Montana of Billings; Daystar, a Native American folklore dance drama ensemble based in Great Falls; and the physically vigorous Aleph Movement Theatre of Helena, which presents new-theater pieces. Polson's Port Polson Players perform comedies suitable for dinner theaters. Shakespeare in the Parks, based in Bozeman, is a professional touring company that performs Shakespearean comedies in full Elizabethan costume. The Montana Repertory Theatre, a professional theater company in residence at the University of Montana in Missoula, tours with plays by regional playwrights.

The Bozeman-based Montana Ballet Company presents both traditional ballet and contemporary dance, with a special commitment to the expression of Montana and Western culture. Earthen Fire Dance Theatre, also of Bozeman, is a contemporary

Every summer, popular shows are presented at the Bigfork Summer Playhouse.

experimental ensemble that combines dance with other artistic media, such as sculpture and poetry.

Summer music and theater events include the Bigfork Summer Playhouse, the Red Lodge Music Festival for high-school students, the University of Montana's Summer Festival of Performing Arts, Montana State University's Adult Chamber Music Festival, the Fort Peck Fine Arts Council's Summer Theatre, the Helena Jazz Festival, the International Dixieland Jazz Festival in Great Falls, the Veterans Day Dixieland Jazz Festival in Missoula, the Big Sky Music Festival, and the International Choral Festival sponsored by Missoula's Mendelssohn Club.

LITERATURE

"Few states can rival the literary production of Montana." That was the opinion of a literary critic after reading *The Last Best Place: A Montana Anthology*. Published in 1989 to celebrate Montana's

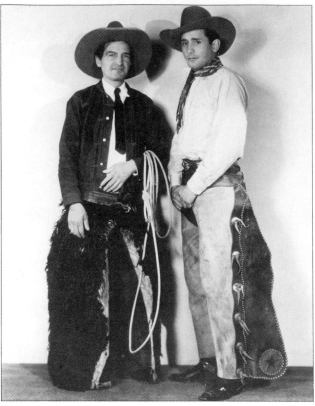

Artists Charles M. Russell (above) and Will
James (on the left in photograph at right)
also wrote tales of Western adventure.

statehood centennial, this enormous collection of Montana
literature brings together stories, poems, and essays ranging from
early Indian tales to modern writings.

Montana's first storytellers were the Indians, who passed on
their histories, myths, and legends orally. Through these ancient
tales, the Indians explain their origins, their moral codes, and the
underlying spirituality of their environment.

Many of Montana's early explorers wrote accounts of their
travels through the territory. The writings of David Thompson,
Meriwether Lewis and William Clark, Henry Edgar, Nathaniel
Langford, and Granville Stuart opened Montana up to armchair
explorers around the world.

Thomas Dimsdale of Virginia City was the first white settler to
publish a book in Montana. His *Vigilantes of Montana, or Popular
Justice in the Rocky Mountains* began in 1865 as a series of articles

in the *Montana Post* and was later published in book form. John Allen Hosmer published Montana's second book, *A Trip to the States*, in 1867, when he was sixteen years old. After spinning an adventurous tale of his trip to Montana, Hosmer printed the book himself on a hand-operated press. In apology for his printing job, Hosmer explained to his readers, ''I had but one small font of type, and scarcely any capitals.''

Later settlers added to Montana's growing body of literature. Mary MacLane of Butte shocked the literary world in 1902 with her highly descriptive personal journal, *The Story of Mary MacLane*. Frank Bird Linderman, who lived near Flathead Lake, transcribed the recollections of two venerable Montana Indians in *Plenty-coups, Chief of the Crows* and *Pretty-shield, Medicine Woman of the Crows*.

Several short stories by Dorothy M. Johnson, who grew up in Whitefish, were made into movies, including ''The Man Who Shot Liberty Valance'' and ''A Man Called Horse.'' Two of Montana's artists, Charles M. Russell and Will James, were also writers. Russell's collection of cowboy stories, *Trails Plowed Under*, appeared in 1937. James's own drawings animate his Western adventure tales *Cowboys North and South*, *Smoky*, and *Lone Cowboy*.

Many prolific writers appeared on Montana's literary scene after World War II. *The Big Sky*, a historical novel by A. B. Guthrie, Jr., of Choteau, became a best-seller after it was published in 1947. Three years later, Guthrie won a Pulitzer Prize for his novel *The Way West*.

Novelist, short-story writer, and essayist Norman Maclean grew up in Montana and spent his later years there until his death in 1990. His 1976 book *A River Runs Through It and Other Stories* is a classic in Montana literature.

Novelist Ivan Doig, in *This House of Sky*, recalls his early years growing up in Montana's Rocky Mountains. Doig's later novels, *Dancing at the Rascal Fair* (1987) and *Ride with Me, Mariah Montana* (1990), round out his Montana historical trilogy.

Novelist and poet James Welch was born to Blackfeet and Gros Ventre parents. In his poetry collection *Riding the Earthboy 40*, his novel *Fools Crow*, and other works, Welch evoked the beauty and dignity of his native people. Poet Richard Hugo gained wide popularity during his tenure at the University of Montana, where he directed the creative writing program.

Many other famous writers moved to Montana in mid-career or spent part of their professional lives in the state. These include Dashiell Hammett, Walter Van Tilburg Clark, Wallace Stegner, Richard Brautigan, and Thomas McGuane.

SPORTS AND RECREATION

Montana has several teams in the Pioneer Baseball League, and many of its college and university campuses have active sports programs. Local and out-of-town sports fans flock to the Washington-Grizzly Stadium at the University of Montana in Missoula. In Bozeman, Montana State University's sporting events include the annual College National Finals Rodeo.

Montana has eleven national forests, two national parks, sixty state parks, and numerous state recreation areas. It is easy to see why most of Montana's sports and recreation activities take place in the great outdoors.

Cars are not allowed in the Bob Marshall Wilderness, the Absaroka-Beartooth Wilderness, and scores of other primitive areas. Loping along the wilderness trails, horseback pack-trippers experience nature in a way they can only describe as spiritual.

A park ranger guiding hikers past a crevasse at Glacier National Park

Hikers, campers, mountain climbers, and wildlife watchers trek these regions, too.

Float-trippers enjoy the scenery along the Missouri, Yellowstone, and other rivers. More adventurous souls prefer white-water rafting in Montana's swift mountain streams.

Montana's rivers and lakes leap with trout, pike, bass, perch, whitefish, and salmon. Ask ten anglers where Montana's best fishing streams are, and they will give ten different answers. Besides the great Yellowstone and Missouri rivers, various sport fishermen swear by the Bighorn, Big Hole, Wise, Madison, Flathead, or Clark Fork rivers. Lake fishermen recommend Boot Jack, Flathead, Georgetown, and Fort Peck lakes. As soon as the lakes freeze, ice fishing begins.

Montana's immense wilderness areas are splendid hunting grounds. There are hunting seasons and quotas for elk, deer, black bears, goats, sheep, moose, ducks, geese, grouse, and pheasant.

In the winter, Montana's mountains and valleys are great for snowmobiling, snowshoeing, and snow skiing. Skiers come from all over the country to experience Montana's "cold smoke," or dry powder snow. Popular ski areas include Big Mountain, near Whitefish; Bridger Bowl, known for its steep slopes and open bowls; and Red Lodge Mountain. Big Sky, southwest of Bozeman, is a lavish resort for wintertime skiing and summertime golfing, fishing, mountain biking, and white-water rafting. West Yellowstone's snowmobile trails have earned it the nickname "snowmobile capital of the world."

Many tourists come to Montana for an offbeat vacation on one of its dude ranches. Lodging on a dude ranch may range from spartan to luxurious, and horses, guides, and riding gear are provided.

For many Montanans, the great range-riding days are still alive. Throughout the year, cowboys come together to match their skills in rodeos. Some of Montana's better-known rodeos are the Wild Horse Stampede rodeo in Wolf Point, the Montana Professional Rodeo Circuit Finals and the State Fair and Rodeo in Great Falls, the Western Montana Fair and Rodeo in Missoula, the Northern International Stock Show and Rodeo in Billings, the Home of Champions Rodeo in Red Lodge, and the Northwest Montana Fair and Rodeo in Kalispell.

Indians on Montana's seven reservations often gather to renew their sense of identity and celebrate their cultural heritage. Their ceremonies, celebrations, and powwows offer colorful and fascinating insights into their ancient cultures. One of the most famous powwows in the nation is the Crow Fair and Rodeo, held

North American Indian Days (left) and the Crow Fair, which includes a rodeo (above), are two exciting annual events in Montana.

every August on the Crow Reservation. Native Americans from all over the United States converge here to compete and to watch exhibitions, filling the site with hundreds of tepees that serve as their temporary homes.

Blackfeet Indians present their North American Indian Days celebration in Browning every July. The Confederated Salish and Kootenai Indians celebrate the Arlee Powwow in early July. Fort Belknap Indian Days are held on the Fort Belknap Reservation in late July. The Northern Cheyenne hold the Ashland Powwow in September and the Northern Cheyenne Powwow at Lame Deer in July.

Assiniboine and Sioux Indians celebrate several festivals on the Fort Peck Reservation. Major events are the Red Bottom Celebration in Frazer, the Wild Horse Stampede in Wolf Point, the Iron Ring Celebration in Poplar, and Wadopanna Powwow near Wolf Point.

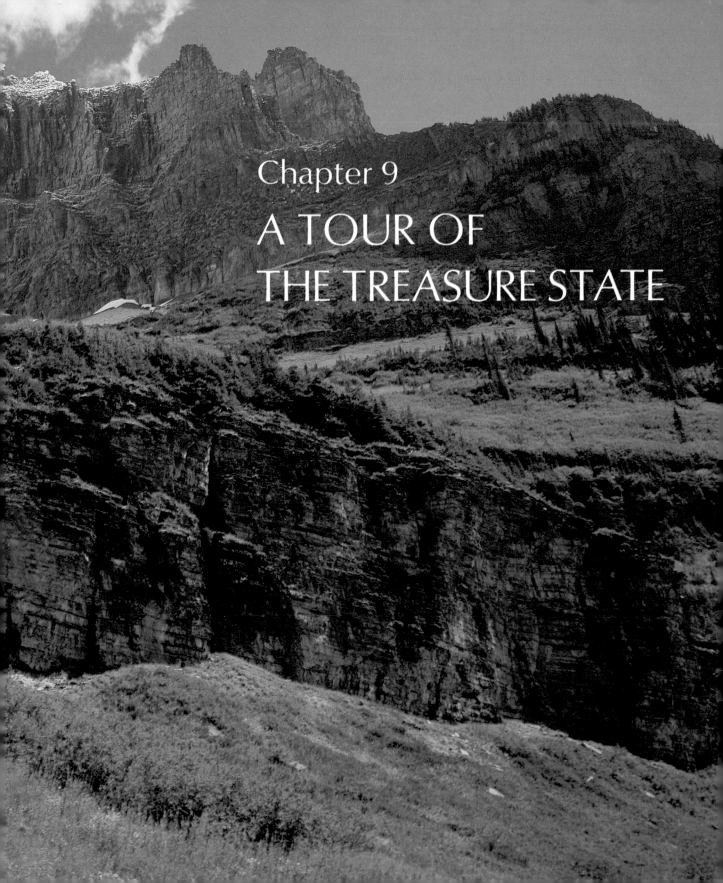

Chapter 9

A TOUR OF
THE TREASURE STATE

A TOUR OF THE TREASURE STATE

For touring convenience, Montana is often divided into six major regions. Each offers a wealth of historical sites and geographical wonders.

SOUTHWESTERN MONTANA

Helena, the state capital, overlooks the Prickly Pear Valley just east of the Continental Divide. The city began as the gold-mining camp of Last Chance Gulch in 1864, and its mushrooming citizenry soon changed the name to the more dignified "Helena." By the 1880s, Helena was reputed to be the richest town in America, home to fifty millionaires. Now smaller and less pretentious, Helena bustles with the business of state government while recalling its earlier days. The city's main street, where mule teams once hauled in miners' supplies, is still called Last Chance Gulch.

Helena's three-story state capitol is built of Montana sandstone and Montana granite. A bronze statue representing Liberty tops the copper dome. Murals by Montana artists Charles M. Russell, Edgar S. Paxson, and Ralph DeCamp decorate the interior. Across the street from the capitol, the Montana Historical Society documents the state's history with its exhibits, archives, and library. The Last Chance Tour Train, departing near the capitol during summer months, takes sightseers past Helena's historic points of interest.

The Original Governor's Mansion, built in 1888, housed nine of Montana's governors between 1913 and 1959. Other historic

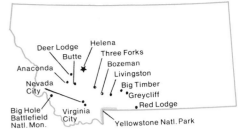

Helena's main street (left) is still called Last Chance Gulch.

nineteenth-century mansions are scattered throughout the city. St. Helena Cathedral, north of the governor's mansion, was modeled after the cathedral in Cologne, Germany. Bishop John P. Carroll laid its cornerstone in 1908. The following year, on a hill on the west side of town, he laid the cornerstone for Carroll College, now one of Montana's three private colleges.

Northeast of Helena, the Missouri River passes narrowly through what Meriwether Lewis called "the most remarkable cliffs that we have yet seen." He named the spot Gates of the Mountains, now the name of the surrounding wilderness area. Visitors here may board tour boats that trace the explorers' route through the magnificent Missouri River Canyon.

In Deer Lodge, west of Helena, is the Montana Territorial Prison. Now a museum, this castlelike stone building was the first territorial prison in the West. Antique Ford automobiles are on display at Deer Lodge's Towe Ford Museum.

Grant-Kohrs Ranch National Historic Site, near Deer Lodge, was once a cattle ranch that covered more than 1 million acres (0.4 million hectares). Today, the 1,564-acre (633-hectare) site includes the original, twenty-three-room Victorian farm mansion and thirty outbuildings.

West of Deer Lodge, State Highway 1 forms a loop called the Pintler Scenic Route. Motorists along the loop are struck by gorgeous views of mountains, forests, and lakes.

In 1883, copper king Marcus Daly founded Anaconda, south of Deer Lodge, and opened his legendary Washoe Smelter and Reduction Works there. The Anaconda Company's smelter, whose smokestack stands 585 feet (178 meters) high, still stands as a formidable reminder of The Company's heyday. Other attractions in and around Anaconda are the cliffs and falls of Lost Creek, the flower gardens of Washoe Park, the 1889 Hearst Free Library, and the National Ghost Town Hall of Fame Museum.

Just a few miles down Interstate 90 from Anaconda is the historic mining town of Butte, where visitors can take a driving tour of old mine sites. A two-hour walking tour winds through the Butte Historic District, with its mansions, union halls, churches, and other notable structures. Copper king William Clark's thirty-room mansion can be toured, and his son Charles's Victorian mansion is now an art museum called the Arts Chateau. The World Museum of Mining, Montana Tech's Mineral Museum, and the ornate St. Lawrence Church are some of Butte's other points of interest.

Southwest of Butte, near the Idaho border, is Big Hole Battlefield National Monument. Visitors there can tour the battlefield where army troops attacked Chief Joseph's band of Nez Perce Indians during their flight from Idaho in 1877.

From Big Hole, a state road arches between two sections of

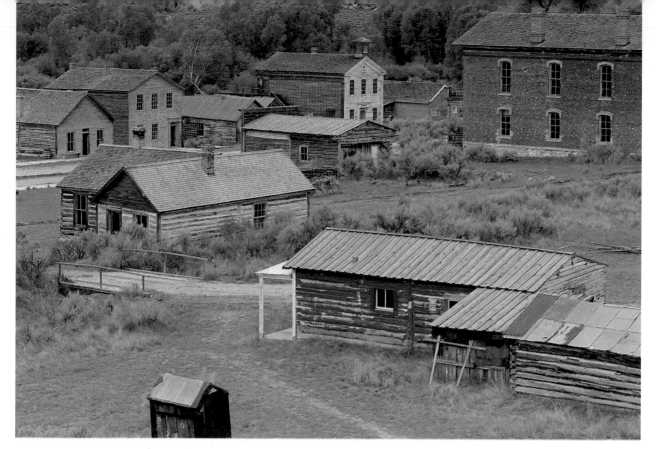
Bannack State Historic Park preserves the site of Montana's first major gold strike.

Beaverhead National Forest to Bannack State Historic Park.
Bannack was the site of Montana's first major gold discovery in
1862. Montana's first territorial capital, Bannack is now a ghost
town whose mining-camp buildings still stand. Walking tours
pass the old jailhouse, the Hotel Meade, and Sheriff Henry
Plummer's gallows.

From Bannack, hardy followers of Lewis and Clark can take a
country road southwest through Lemhi Pass, where the explorers
crossed the Continental Divide.

East of Butte, toward Three Forks, is Lewis and Clark Caverns
State Park, one of the largest limestone caverns in the Northwest.
About an hour's drive south of the cavern are the old mining
towns of Nevada City and Virginia City. In 1863, the world's

Historic buildings in the old mining towns of Virginia City (left) and Nevada City (right) remind visitors of Montana's boomtown days.

richest placer gold discovery was made in Virginia City. Today the restored boomtown has more than twenty historic buildings.

Madison Canyon Earthquake Area, southeast of Virginia City, is a startling reminder of Montana's 1959 earthquake. Here, 80 million tons (73 million metric tons) of rock—half a mountain—slid into the Madison River, creating Quake Lake.

SOUTH-CENTRAL MONTANA

Bozeman, on Interstate 90 east of Butte, is the home of Montana State University. The campus's Museum of the Rockies traces four billion years of northern Rocky Mountain history. Dinosaur exhibits, western art, Indian artifacts, and a planetarium are just a few of the museum's spectacular features.

Bozeman is a convenient jumping-off point for travelers in search of mystery, beautiful scenery, or fun. It is the headquarters for the Montana Wilderness Foundation, which conducts trips into the state's many wilderness areas, and also the headquarters for the Gallatin National Forest to the south.

Spectacular Yellowstone National Park is about a two-hour drive south of Bozeman. Although most of Yellowstone lies in Wyoming, three of the park's five entrances are in Montana. On Montana highways, park visitors can enter from the west at West Yellowstone, from the north at Gardiner, and from the east at Cooke City/Silver Gate.

Yellowstone was the world's first national park, and many visitors believe it is the most eerie. Nowhere else on earth can one see such bizarre geological sights as Yellowstone's bubbling mineral pools and spewing geysers.

West of Bozeman on Interstate 90 is Three Forks, where the Jefferson, Madison, and Gallatin rivers meet to form the Missouri River. Hikers, campers, and fishermen enjoy the natural surroundings of Missouri Headwaters State Park. Mysterious prehistoric pictographs, or picture writings, can be seen on stones along some of the park's hiking trails. Southwest of town is Madison Buffalo Jump State Historic Site, where Indians stampeded bison over the cliffs more than two thousand years ago.

Southwest of Bozeman is a recreational complex called Big Sky. Besides being a wintertime ski resort, Big Sky offers white-water rafting, tennis, mountain biking, and other summer recreation.

East of Bozeman is Livingston, whose downtown area is a national historic district. Livingston's Depot Center is a restored railroad station, displaying a large art and history exhibit from the Buffalo Bill Historical Center in Cody, Wyoming.

Fall color along the Yellowstone River north of Corwin Springs

The drive south from Livingston is the most direct route to Yellowstone National Park. From Livingston, U.S. Highway 89 follows the Yellowstone River south through Paradise Valley into the park. Along Yellowstone Park's northern border is the Absaroka-Beartooth Wilderness, where no automobile traffic is allowed. Serious hikers and horseback riders spend their vacations exploring this rugged terrain. Granite Peak, Montana's highest point, is one of the wilderness's twenty-eight mountains that rise over 12,000 feet (3,658 meters).

The eastern approach to Yellowstone is a more out-of-the-way route than the others, but its scenery makes the drive worthwhile. Beartooth Highway—U.S. Highway 212—leads from Red Lodge right into Yellowstone at Cooke City/Silver Gate. Charles Kuralt, television's traveling reporter, has called the Beartooth Highway

Rock Tree Canyon in the Beartooth Mountains near Red Lodge

"the most beautiful drive in America." It takes about three hours to drive this 69-mile (111-kilometer) road, but the slow pace has its rewards. Glaciers, snowy peaks, and alpine meadows greet the eye along the route.

In Red Lodge, the Red Lodge Historic District around Main Street preserves many homes and other buildings from the town's turn-of-the-century coal-mining days. Miners from many European countries came to work the mines, and their ethnic neighborhoods are still scattered through town. Red Lodge's nine-day Festival of Nations, in August, highlights a different nation's food, crafts, and music each day.

Big Timber, east of Livingston, holds the Montana Cowboy Poetry Gathering every August. Here poets and musicians gather to share their poems and ballads of life on the range. Southwest of Big Timber, at Natural Bridge, one sees the spectacular falls and canyon of the Boulder River. To the east, a community of hardy little rodents thrives in Greycliff's Prairie Dog Town.

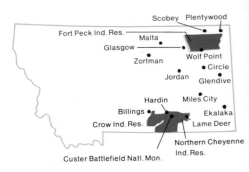

Billings, Montana's largest city, lies in the south-central part of the state.

SOUTHEASTERN MONTANA

Billings, Montana's largest city, is a bustling metropolitan area on Montana's Great Plains. Modern-day ranchers ship their livestock through Billings just as many others have done for the last century. Converging air, rail, and highway routes make the city a major transportation hub. Visitors to Billings can choose from a variety of cultural events, museums, galleries, and shopping areas. The Alberta Bair Theater, Montana's largest performing-arts center, hosts over one hundred local and touring events every year. The Billings Historic District includes the Carlin Hotel, with its theater pipe organ; and the Rex Hotel, built with the help of Buffalo Bill Cody. Visitors to Billings may also tour the campuses of Eastern Montana College and Rocky Mountain College.

94

From Billings, it is easy to reach many of the area's fascinating historic sites. Pictograph Cave State Historic Site, southeast of Billings, features the remains of a five-thousand-year-old prehistoric culture. Thousands of tools and household implements have been found here, and visitors can view ancient pictographs near the cave.

Southeast of Billings is the large Crow Indian Reservation. Its Crow Fair, held in August, is one of the largest and most famous powwows in the country. At Hardin, on the reservation's northern edge, is Big Horn County Historical Museum and Visitor Center. On the reservation south of Pryor is Chief Plenty Coups State Historic Park. Plenty Coups, the last of the great Crow chiefs, lived in the log cabin there and was buried nearby.

South of Hardin, in the Little Bighorn River Valley, is Custer Battlefield National Monument. This is the site of the Sioux and Cheyenne victory over Lieutenant Colonel George Custer in 1876. The battle is periodically reenacted there. Some people claim to have seen the spirits of fallen Indians roaming across the desolate battle site.

Rosebud Battlefield, to the southeast, is the site of one of the largest Indian battles in United States history. The 1876 battle between the Sioux and General Crook's troops took place just eight days before Custer's fall at the Little Bighorn.

The Northern Cheyenne reservation adjoins the Crow reservation on the east. Lame Deer, the tribal headquarters, hosts the Northern Cheyenne Powwow in early July. The reservation's Cheyenne Indian Museum includes the Little Coyote Gallery of Indian artwork.

Bighorn Canyon National Recreation Area overlaps the southwestern part of the Crow reservation. One of Montana's most popular recreation areas, it surrounds limestone-walled

Bighorn Canyon. Yellowtail Dam, 525 feet (160 meters) high, harnesses the Bighorn River to create 71-mile-long (114-kilometer-long) Bighorn Lake within the canyon. West of Bighorn Canyon is Pryor Mountains National Wild Horse Range. Running free in these mountains are about 130 wild mustangs, thought to be descended from a herd that arrived in the 1700s.

East of Billings, Interstate 94 parallels the Yellowstone River. About a half-hour's drive leads to Pompey's Pillar, a massive sandstone rock named after Sacagawea's son. In 1806, William Clark carved his signature—still visible—in this stone. Rock hunters can be seen browsing alongside the Yellowstone River from this point eastward to the North Dakota border. These riverbanks have yielded dazzling agates, as well as jaspers, fossils, and petrified wood.

Farther east is Miles City, named for Indian fighter Nelson Miles. Texas longhorn cattle drives used to end up in Miles City, and the residents' cowboy attire still lends the town a Western flavor. Miles City holds a rodeo every May, with wild-horse races and a world-famous bucking-horse auction. L. A. Huffman's photographs of early buffalo herds and frontier scenes hang in Coffrin's Old West Gallery on Main Street.

The Range Riders Museum on the west side of town includes the town's old Main Street, army officers' quarters, and a huge gun collection. Outside of town is Fort Keogh, named after a captain who fell with Custer at the Battle of Little Bighorn. Once one of the largest cavalry posts in Montana, the fort maintains several buildings and its parade grounds.

A side trip east of Miles City leads to Montana's desolate badlands. Just north of Ekalaka is Medicine Rocks State Park, an area of strangely eroded sandstone rock formations where Indian hunters once called upon magic spirits. Ekalaka's Carter County

Unusual rock formations can be seen at Makoshika State Park.

Museum contains an extensive collection of fossils, including an Antosaurus (duck-billed dinosaur) skeleton.

Makoshika State Park near Glendive offers more of the badlands' bizarre scenery. *Makoshika* is the Sioux word for "bad earth" or "bad land." Vultures soar over the landscape, once the home of the Tyrannosaur and Triceratops.

From Glendive, near the eastern border, travelers can embark on a tour of the wild and scenic Missouri River country.

NORTHEASTERN MONTANA

Fort Union, at the North Dakota border north of Sidney, was a bustling fur-trading post and Missouri River port in the mid-1800s. Indians, boatmen, wealthy traders, and grizzled trappers mingled together at Fort Union, now a national historic site.

Fort Union, now a national historic site, was an important Missouri River fur-trading post in the mid-1800s.

North of Fort Union, Medicine Lake National Wildlife Refuge shelters dozens of species of waterfowl and game animals. White pelicans and whooping cranes are regular residents, while as many as 250,000 migrating birds stop by in the spring and fall.

In the northeast corner of the state, Plentywood's Sheridan County Museum exhibits antique tractors and threshing machines. More pioneer farm machinery is on display in Scobey, west of Plentywood, among the homes and shops of the Restored Pioneer Town of the 1900s. In July, Scobey holds a threshing bee and antique show.

North of the Missouri River, between Culbertson and Nashua, is Fort Peck Indian Reservation, home of Sioux and Assiniboine Indians. Visitors get a glimpse of the Indians' tribal culture at celebrations such as the Wild Horse Stampede in Wolf Point,

Wadopanna Powwow nearby, and the Iron Ring Celebration in Poplar. Wolf Point's rodeo, held in July, has been running since 1901.

About an hour's drive west of Wolf Point is Fort Peck Dam, one of the largest in the world. Stretching westward from the dam is scenic Fort Peck Lake, with its 1,600 miles (2,575 kilometers) of shoreline. The Charles M. Russell National Wildlife Refuge surrounds the entire lake. Deer, antelope, bighorn sheep, waterfowl, and other wildlife abound in the refuge's prairies, badlands, and river bottoms.

A country road north from Jordan leads to the fossil beds on Hell Creek, alongside Fort Peck Lake. This is the site where paleontologists discovered a nearly complete skeleton of the fierce, carnivorous Tyrannosaurus Rex.

Farther west, the UL Bend Wilderness juts into Fort Peck Lake. This prairie-covered peninsula, created by glacial movements, is the primitive wilderness home for elk, deer, pronghorn antelope, and other wild animals.

Many towns north and south of Fort Peck Lake maintain historical museums. The McCone County Museum in Circle illustrates the area's history through Indian artifacts, firearms, homesteaders' implements, and a wildlife collection. Glasgow's Pioneer Museum displays fossils, Indian materials, and historical objects from the area's early railroad and businesses. Other museums in the region include the Garfield County Museum in Jordan and the Phillips County Historical Museum in Malta.

South of U.S. Highway 2 on the way to Malta is the Bowdoin National Wildlife Refuge. Here, photographers and nature watchers can stalk deer, antelope, and more than two hundred species of birds. Southwest of Malta, near Zortman, the Little Rocky Mountains jut upward from the plains. These mineral-rich hills have yielded precious sapphires and over $25 million worth of gold. At Pegasus Gold's Zortman Mine, guided tours lead visitors through a modern gold mine.

Continuing west from Malta, one enters the land of plains, buttes, and endless skies that cowboy artist Charlie Russell loved and painted.

NORTH-CENTRAL MONTANA

The Fort Belknap Indian Reservation, headquartered at Fort Belknap Agency, is home to Montana's Gros Ventre and Assiniboine Indians. West of the reservation and south of Chinook is the Chief Joseph Battleground. This is the site where Chief Joseph of the Nez Perce surrendered in 1877 after a 1,700-mile (2,736-kilometer) flight and a six-day battle with U.S. Army troops.

Farther west, in Havre, is the Wahkpa Chu'gn Archaeology Site, the largest bison-kill site in this part of the Great Plains.

U.S. Highway 87 cuts southwest from Havre to meet the Missouri River at Fort Benton. Rich with history, this town was once a fur-trading post, an army fort, and the head of Missouri River steamboat navigation. The museum and historic buildings of Fort Benton Landmark District preserve Fort Benton's history. The town's Montana Agriculture Center and Museum of the Northern Great Plains illustrates the area's farming history through early farm machinery, a homestead village, and library and archive materials.

From Fort Benton, the Upper Missouri National Wild and Scenic River extends 150 miles (241 kilometers) down the Missouri River. Boarding a boat at Fort Benton, tourists can follow the route of Lewis and Clark as they explored and camped along

Citadel Rock was one of the landmarks along Lewis and Clark's route through Montana.

the riverbanks. The tour passes their camp at Slaughter Creek, as well as Citadel Rock, Hole in the Wall, and the scenic White Cliffs area.

At Great Falls, upriver from Fort Benton, Lewis and Clark spent twenty-five treacherous days portaging around the Great Falls of the Missouri. Today, the Great Falls Chamber of Commerce issues ''The Explorers at the Portage,'' an interpretive map of the expedition's portage route. The Lewis and Clark Trail Heritage Foundation provides more information about the expedition. Five dams now harness the power of these mighty falls.

Great Falls is also famous as the home of Montana's beloved artist Charles M. Russell. In the C. M. Russell Museum complex are his original home and log-cabin studio, as well as an extensive collection of his works. Every March, Great Falls hosts the Charles M. Russell art auction, a massive sale of fine Western art.

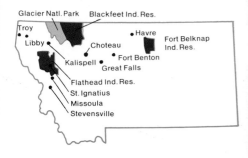

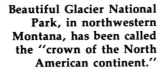

Beautiful Glacier National Park, in northwestern Montana, has been called the "crown of the North American continent."

Other points of interest in Great Falls are Mehmke's Steam Engine Museum, the Cascade County Historical Museum, the Montana Cowboys Association Museum, and the campus of the College of Great Falls.

On the northwest edge of Great Falls is Giant Springs Heritage State Park, where William Clark came upon an enormous spring while portaging around the falls. One of the largest springs in the world, it puts out 270,000 gallons (1,022,058 liters) of water a minute, or about 390 million gallons (1.5 billion liters) a day.

West of Great Falls is Ulm Pishkun, an ancient buffalo jump site. Stretching for about a mile (1.6 kilometers), it is believed to be the largest prehistoric bison-kill site in the country.

Northwest of Great Falls is Choteau, named for the fur-trading Chouteau family. (The surrounding county was named "Chouteau," and the *u* was dropped from the town's name so the two would not be confused.) Choteau's Old Trail Museum

Iceberg Lake
at Glacier
National Park

displays fossils, Indian artifacts, and pioneer gear. The museum's
dinosaur fossil beds are located just outside of town.

NORTHWESTERN MONTANA

Montana's northwest corner is a land of majestic mountains,
towering glaciers, wild rivers, and glistening lakes. Glacier
National Park crowns the northern border, while a number of
national wilderness areas are scattered throughout the region: Bob
Marshall, Great Bear, Cabinets, Rattlesnake, Selway-Bitterroot,
Welcome Creek, Missions, and Anaconda-Pintler.

At the Canadian boundary, Glacier National Park adjoins
Alberta's Waterton Lakes National Park. Together, the parks form
Waterton-Glacier International Peace Park. Visitors to Glacier
National Park find a scenic wonderland of glaciers, lakes, streams,
wildflowers, waterfalls, forests, and wildlife. More than fifty

The Blackfeet Indian Reservation lies adjacent to Glacier National Park.

glaciers lie above glassy lakes and wildflower-covered valleys. Mountain goats, bighorn sheep, grizzly bears, and gray wolves roam freely through the park. With nearly 1,000 miles (1,609 kilometers) of trails, Glacier is a hikers' paradise. Motorists may cross the Continental Divide at Logan Pass on the 55-mile (89-kilometer) Going-to-the-Sun Road.

Bordering Glacier National Park to the east is the Blackfeet Indian Reservation, home of the largest Indian tribe in the state. The Museum of the Plains Indians, on the reservation in Browning, features a fabulous collection of Blackfeet artifacts and traces the history of Northern Great Plains Indians.

Glacier National Park's western boundary is the North Fork of the Flathead River. Along with the middle and south forks, it forms the Flathead National Wild and Scenic River system. Coursing through 219 miles (352 kilometers) of rugged wilderness, this is one of the longest wild-and-scenic river systems in the country.

Flathead Lake is Montana's largest natural lake.

South of Glacier National Park and the Blackfeet Reservation is the Bob Marshall Wilderness. The second-largest wilderness area in the country, it straddles the Continental Divide and can be traversed only by trails. Together, the Bob Marshall, Scapegoat, and Great Bear wildernesses encompass more than 1.5 million acres (607,035 hectares) of rugged land.

Pioneer trader C. E. Conrad founded the city of Kalispell, southwest of Glacier Park, and his restored Victorian mansion is still there. A drive west of Kalispell leads to the Cabinet Mountains Wilderness and on to Libby Dam, which backs up Lake Koocanusa. Kootenai Falls, between Libby and Troy, was a sacred spot for the Kootenai Indians. In the Giant Cedars-Ross Creek Scenic Area south of Troy, five-hundred-year-old cedar trees soar over 250 feet (76 meters) above walking trails.

Flathead Lake, south of Kalispell, is the West's largest natural freshwater lake. Its southern shores cut into the Flathead Indian Reservation, home of the Salish and Kootenai Indians. In the reservation town of St. Ignatius stands St. Ignatius Mission, built by Jesuit missionaries in 1854. Fifty-eight murals by artistic missionary Brother Joseph Carignano adorn the mission's walls and ceilings.

Across U.S. Highway 93 from St. Ignatius, near Moiese, is the National Bison Range. This is the grazing ground for about four hundred American bison—one of the last bison herds in the United States. Visitors driving through the 19,000-acre (7,689-hectare) range may also spot pronghorn antelope, elk, and deer grazing the grasslands.

The city of Missoula lies in the basin of a prehistoric lake. Around it rise the Sapphire and Bitterroot mountains, and the Clark Fork of the Columbia River cuts through the center of town. Mount Lolo, Mount Jumbo, Mount Sentinel, and Squaw Peak loom on the city's horizons. According to one story, Salish Indians gave Missoula its name, calling the place *Im-i-sul-a*—"by the chilling water."

The University of Montana was founded in Missoula in 1893, and its campus remains a lively cultural and sports center. Caras Park, along the riverfront, is a popular recreation area and the home of the university's summer theater.

Historic structures recall Missoula's pioneer days while revealing Montana's artistic heritage. Eight murals by Edgar Paxson relate events in Montana's history in the block-long Missoula County Courthouse. Built in 1889 and topped by a graceful steeple, St. Francis Xavier Church features Joseph Carignano's elaborate paintings. The Wilma Theatre, fascinating to architecture buffs, saw many live music and drama shows in its day.

On the southwest side of town is the Historical Museum at Fort Missoula, a complex of twelve historic buildings. The corrals and blacksmith shop at Ninemile Remount Depot, west of Missoula,

Missoula's historic County Courthouse (left) and Clark Fork Station (right)

were used to outfit pack animals for fire fighters to ride. Modern-day Forest Service smoke jumpers are headquartered at the Aerial Fire Depot, also west of town.

Residents of Missoula can escape northward to the vast Rattlesnake National Recreation Area and Wilderness for hiking, camping, and other recreation. Northwest of Missoula is the popular Snow Bowl ski resort, which also offers 7,000-foot (2,134-meter) chair-lift rides in the summer.

Stevensville, south of Missoula, is the site of St. Mary's Misson, founded by Father De Smet in 1841. Visitors to Hamilton, south of Stevensville, can tour copper king Marcus Daly's elegant, forty-two-room mansion.

Montana's minerals gave it the nickname Treasure State. For residents and visitors alike, however, the Big Sky Country's true wealth is the magnificent sweep of its land.

FACTS AT A GLANCE

GENERAL INFORMATION

Statehood: November 8, 1889, forty-first state

Origin of Name: The name *Montana* is derived from the Spanish word for "mountainous"

State Capital: Helena, begun as Last Chance Gulch in 1864 and incorporated as Helena in 1881

State Nickname: Montana has several nicknames. The rich mineral resources of its western mountain region have earned it the nickname "Treasure State." The state is also called "Big Sky Country" and the "Last Best Place."

State Flag: Montana's state flag features a version of the state seal on a field of dark blue, with the word *Montana* emblazoned in gold across the top. The flag was adopted in 1905, and modifications were added in 1981 and 1985. Colonel Harry C. Kessler, who led the First Montana Infantry volunteers into the Spanish-American War in 1898, first used the banner as his unit's insignia. In 1981, the word *Montana* was added, and the exact colors for the flag's seal were established: gold sky with white clouds and white sun rays, and blue-and-white waterfalls. In 1985, the state legislature declared Helvetica Bold as the official style of lettering for the word *Montana*.

State Motto: *Oro y Plata*, Spanish for "Gold and Silver"

State Bird: Western meadowlark

State Animal: Grizzly bear

State Fish: Black-spotted cutthroat trout

State Flower: Bitterroot

State Tree: Ponderosa pine

State Gemstones: Sapphire and agate

State Grass: Bluebunch wheatgrass

State Fossil: Duck-billed dinosaur (*Maiasaura peeblesorum*)

State Song and State Ballad: In 1935, the state legislature adopted "Montana," with words by Charles C. Cohan and music by Joseph E. Howard, as the official state song. In a 1983 compromise, the legislature adopted "Montana Melody," with words by LeGrande and Carleen Harvey and music by LeGrande Harvey, as the state ballad.

MONTANA

Tell me of that Treasure State
Story always new,
Tell of its beauties grand
And its hearts so true.

Mountains of sunset fire
The land I love the best
Let me grasp the hand of one
From out the golden West.

Chorus:
Montana, Montana,
Glory of the West
Of all the states from coast to coast,
You're easily the best.
Montana, Montana,
Where skies are always blue
M - O - N - T - A - N - A,
Montana, I love you.

Each country has its flow'r;
Each one plays a part,
Each bloom brings a longing hope
To some lonely heart.

Bitter Root to me is dear
Growing in my land
Sing then that glorious air
The one I understand.

(Chorus)

MONTANA MELODY

I long to be in the places that I see
in the pictures of my dreams
Where there's mountains full of trees,
meadows carpeted in green
Silent, snow-fall, clear running streams.

Where the bear-grass blooms
In the spring-time of the year,
And the larch turn gold in the Fall
Where there's deer, elk and antelope
Beaver, bears and birds and the yippin'
coyotes serenade them all.

Chorus:
Yes, there's no place like Montana,
the Big Sky country, my home.
A place to set my spirit free,
a Rocky Mountain melody,
These things are a part of me,
Montana, Montana, my home.

Charlie Russell clouds paint sunsets in the West,
in colors of red, blue and gold.
Snow-capped peaks reach endless to the sky,
and the grain-fields with gentle breezes flow.

There's high mountain lakes, Missouri river breaks
and the open plains, where the buffalo used to roam.
It's a cowboy song, it's where Indians belong
God's country, my home sweet home.

I had a dream, of how Heaven's s'posed to be,
and when I die, that's where I want to go.
Cause there's mountains full of trees, meadows
carpeted in green, silent snowfall, clear running
streams.

(Chorus)

POPULATION

Population: 799,065, forty-fourth among the states (1990 census)

Population Density: 5.5 people per sq. mi. (2 people per km²)

Population Distribution: 53 percent of the people live in cities or towns.

Billings	81,151
Great Falls	55,097
Missoula	42,918
Butte-Silver Bow	33,336
Helena	24,569
Bozeman	22,660
Kalispell	11,917

(Population figures according to 1990 census)

Population Growth: The discovery of silver and gold was the major factor in Montana's early population growth. The number of Montanans almost doubled in the 1870s. During the mining rush of the 1880s, Montana's overall population increased 265 percent. In the same decade, the state's urban areas—including mining towns such as Butte—grew 455 percent. The state continued to draw large numbers of new residents until the 1920s, when the population dropped 2 percent. Population recovery was well underway in the years after World War II. The 1950s brought a 14 percent increase; the 1970s, a 13 percent increase; and the 1980s, a 5 percent increase. The list below shows population growth in Montana since 1870:

Year	Population
1870	20,595
1880	39,159
1890	142,924
1900	243,329
1920	548,889
1930	537,606
1940	559,456
1950	591,024
1960	674,767
1970	694,409
1980	786,690
1990	799,065

GEOGRAPHY

Borders: On Montana's northern border are the Canadian provinces of British Columbia, Alberta, and Saskatchewan. Montana is bordered by the states of North Dakota and South Dakota on the east, Idaho on the west, and Idaho and Wyoming on the south.

Highest Point: Granite Peak, 12,799 ft. (3,901 m)

Lowest Point: Lincoln County along the Kootenai River, 1,820 ft. (555 m)

Greatest Distances: North to south—321 mi. (517 km)
East to west—559 mi. (900 km)

Area: 147,046 sq. mi. (380,849 km²)

Rank in Area Among the States: Fourth

Indian Lands: While Montana has seven Indian reservations, land is also allotted to individual Indian families. About 5 percent of Montana's population consists of members of ten Indian groups, who are concentrated in and around the state's reservations. Kootenai and Salish Indians live on the Flathead Reservation, Piegan Blackfeet reside at the Blackfeet Reservation around Browning, Gros Ventres and Assiniboine occupy the Fort Belknap Reservation, Sioux and Assiniboine live at the Fort Peck Reservation, Northern Cheyenne reside on the Northern Cheyenne Reservation at Lame Deer, Crow Indians live on the Crow Reservation south of Hardin, and Chippewa and Cree occupy Rocky Boy's Reservation near Havre.

Rivers: The Missouri and Yellowstone rivers are Montana's most important rivers. Both flow eastward from the western mountains. The Yellowstone is the geologically older of the two. Its alluvial plain is wider than the Missouri's. Together, the two river systems drain about 85 percent of the state's land area. The Missouri River begins near the town of Three Forks, at the juncture of the Madison, Jefferson, and Gallatin rivers. From there, the Missouri follows a great northerly arc, flowing past Helena and through a gorge called Gates of the Mountains. The Missouri then continues eastward into North Dakota. In northeastern Montana, Fort Peck Dam on the Missouri River forms Fort Peck Lake. Major tributaries of the Missouri include the Milk, Musselshell, Marias, Sun, and Teton rivers. The Milk River extends north into Canada.

The more southerly Yellowstone River flows eastward across the state from Yellowstone National Park, eventually joining the Missouri River in North Dakota, just past the Montana border. The Yellowstone's major branches include the Bighorn, Powder, Tongue, and Shields rivers. Western Montana's major river is the Clark Fork of the Columbia River. It rises near Butte on the western slope of the Continental Divide, not far from the Three Forks of the Missouri. The Blackfoot, Bitterroot, Flathead, and Thompson rivers are the Clark Fork's major branches. Joining the Clark Fork in British Columbia is the Kootenai River, which cuts across Montana's northwest corner.

Lakes: Flathead Lake is Montana's largest natural lake, covering about 189 sq. mi. (490 km²). It is also the largest natural freshwater lake west of the Mississippi River. Missoula Lake, now dry, was once a large glacial lake. Glaciers have formed hundreds of other lakes in the Glacier National Park region, though most are relatively small. Fort Peck Lake, backed up by Fort Peck Dam on the

A waterfall in northwestern Montana

Missouri River, is the state's largest artificially created body of water. Other artificial lakes include Hungry Horse Reservoir, Bighorn Lake, Canyon Ferry Lake, and Tiber Reservoir. Lake Koocanusa, formed by Libby Dam on the Kootenai River, lies partly in British Columbia, Canada. It provides hydroelectric power and flood control for residents on both sides of the border.

Topography: Montana is divided into two land regions. The eastern three-fifths of the state is part of the Great Plains region; the western two-fifths is part of the Rocky Mountain region. The rolling plains of the Great Plains region, once covered with tall, waving grasses, are now carpeted with sagebrush and shortgrass. Wheat farming and cattle ranching flourish on Montana's plains. Rising sharply from the plains are a number of low mountains, including the Bears Paw, Highwood, Big Snowy, Judith, and Little Rocky mountains. The state's best farmland lies along the Yellowstone River Valley and in the "Golden Triangle" region of north-central Montana. In far-eastern Montana, wind and water erosion along the Yellowstone and other rivers have created badlands. The badlands are characterized by severe trenches, arid soil, and colorful rock formations.

A snow-covered field in the Gallatin Valley near Bozeman

The mountain ranges of the Rocky Mountain region run generally northwest to southeast. The more than fifty Rocky Mountain ranges in Montana include the Bitterroot, Mission, Flathead, Lewis, and Swan ranges in the west; the Bridger, Gallatin, Madison, Tobacco Root, and Ruby ranges in the southwest; and, in the central part of the state, the Big Belt, Little Belt, Crazy, and Pryor mountains.

A ridgeline known as the Continental Divide zigzags through the western mountains, marking the division between North America's Great Plains and its Pacific coastal region. From Glacier National Park in the north, this jagged line runs south through the Flathead mountain range, then cuts westward to form part of the border between Montana and Idaho, and continues into Yellowstone National Park in the south. The Continental Divide is North America's major watershed; rivers generally flow west from its western face and east down its eastern slopes.

Climate: Because of Montana's geographical diversity, its climate is also diverse. The climate west of the Continental Divide is generally more temperate and the precipitation (moisture such as rain and snow) heavier. The divide protects the western region from severe Canadian winds and also captures the moisture from winds blowing from the west. January temperatures average 20°F. (-7°C) in the west and 14°F. (-10°C) in the east. In July, the western mountains average 64°F. (18°C), while the east averages 71°F. (22°C). Both Glendive and Medicine Lake

114

experienced the state's highest recorded temperature of 117°F. (47°C). Glendive reached that temperature on July 20, 1893, and Medicine Lake matched it on July 5, 1937.

In the winter, the eastern plains are sometimes plagued by severe blizzards, and fierce winds from Canada can whip down across the plains. However, warm, dry winter winds called *chinooks* also gust down from the eastern slopes of the Continental Divide. The lowest temperature ever recorded in Montana was -70°F. (-57°C), at Rogers Pass on January 20, 1954. This was also, at the time, the lowest temperature ever recorded in the forty-eight contiguous states. Although temperatures are more extreme in the east, the drier air makes them less uncomfortable. The heaviest rains fall in the spring and early summer, and the heaviest snowfalls occur in the mountains. Excluding the far west, Montana's average precipitation statewide is 13 to 14 in. (33 to 36 cm) a year. More than 34 in. (86 cm) of moisture falls on Heron, in the far northwest.

NATURE

Trees: Alders, ashes, aspens, birches, western red cedars, cottonwoods, lowland white and Douglas firs, western hemlocks, junipers, western larches (tamaracks), lodgepole pines, ponderosa (western yellow) pines, western white pines, willows, Engelmann spruces

Wild Plants: Arnicas, asters, bear grass, bitterroots, blue grama, bluebells, bluegrasses, bulrushes, cacti, cattails, columbines, currants, daisies, dryads, globeflowers, gooseberries, Oregon grapes, heathers, huckleberries, Indian paintbrushes, kinnikinnick, Labrador teas, Rocky Mountain laurels, lilies, lupines, green needlegrass, poppies, primroses, Russian wild rye, sagebrush, serviceberries, violets, wheatgrasses, windflowers, yellow bells, yuccas

Animals: Pronghorn antelope, axolotls, black bears, grizzly bears, beavers, coyotes, mule deer, white-tailed deer, elk, mountain goats, gophers, jackrabbits, minks, moose, mountain sheep, muskrats, rattlesnakes, weasels, wolves

Birds: Blackbirds, bobolinks, chickadees, ducks, geese, grouse, juncoes, magpies, meadowlarks, partridges, pheasants

Fish: Catfish, crappie, grayling, perch, pike, salmon, sturgeon, sunfish, trout, whitefish

GOVERNMENT

The government of Montana, like the federal government, is divided into three branches: legislative, executive, and judicial. The state legislature makes the state laws. Like the United States Congress, Montana's legislature consists of two houses: a senate and a house of representatives. State legislators are elected by voters in Montana's senatorial and representative districts. The fifty state senators are elected to four-year terms; one-half of them are elected every two years. The one hundred state representatives serve two-year terms. In accordance with a 1974 constitutional amendment, Montana's legislature meets for regular sessions on the first Monday in January of odd-numbered years and may remain in session for up to ninety workdays. The governor or the legislators may also call special sessions. After the legislature passes a bill into law, the governor either approves or vetoes it. By a two-thirds vote in both houses, the legislature may override the governor's veto.

The governor is the head of the executive branch, which enforces state laws. Voters elect the governor to serve a four-year term; the governor may be reelected any number of times. Other executive officers, all elected to four-terms, are the lieutenant governor, secretary of state, attorney general, superintendent of public instruction, state auditor, and public service commissioners. The governor appoints the heads of seventeen executive departments and several state institutions.

The judicial branch interprets the law and tries cases. The state's highest court is the supreme court. Its chief justice and six associate justices are elected by popular vote for eight-year terms. Judges in Montana's twenty district courts are elected for six-year terms. They try major civil and criminal cases. At the local level, each county elects at least one justice of the peace to serve a four-year term presiding over a justice court. Many towns also have municipal and police courts.

Number of Counties: 56, plus a part of Yellowstone National Park

U.S. Representatives: 1

Electoral Votes: 3

Voting Qualifications: 18 years of age

EDUCATION

Montana's first schools were opened in Bannack and Nevada City in 1863. In the winter of 1863-64, Thomas Dimsdale taught the children of Virginia City, charging $2 a week for tuition. In 1864, the Jesuit mission at St. Ignatius opened a boarding school for Indian children, taught by the Sisters of Providence from Montreal. In the following decade, a number of schools were opened in Montana, some run by religious groups and others operated by subscription. In 1865, the territorial legislature established a public school system, organized by Judge Cornelius Hedges. The legislature of the new state of Montana instituted a state board of education in 1893 and provided for free county schools in 1897.

Today, about 75 percent of the adults in Montana are high-school graduates. The state's literacy rate is high, about 92 percent. State law requires children between the ages of eight and sixteen to attend school. Montana has about 774 public elementary and secondary schools in 550 school districts. There are also about 105 private elementary and secondary schools in the state. Schools made up mainly of Indian students are required to provide instruction in Indian culture.

Six four-year colleges and universities, five vocational technical centers, and three public community colleges comprise Montana's public higher-education system. The state colleges and universities are Montana State University in Bozeman, the University of Montana in Missoula, Eastern Montana College in Billings, Western Montana College in Dillon, Northern Montana College in Havre, and the College of Mineral Science and Technology in Butte. Montana also has three private colleges: Carroll College in Helena and the College of Great Falls in Great Falls, both run by the Roman Catholic church; and Rocky Mountain College in Billings, jointly operated by the Congregational, Methodist, and Presbyterian churches. Indian students are enrolled in Montana's public and private colleges, as well as in the state's seven tribally controlled community colleges.

ECONOMY AND INDUSTRY

Principal Products:
Agriculture: Beef cattle, wheat, hay, barley, oats, rye, flaxseed, potatoes, sugar beets, hogs, sheep, wool, milk, poultry, eggs, honey, black cherries

Manufacturing: Lumber and wood products, beet sugar, meat products, flour, petroleum and coal products, copper products, aluminum products, farm machinery, fabricated metal products, fertilizers, printed materials, cement, stone and clay products, glass products

Natural Resources: Petroleum, coal, natural gas, gold, silver, copper, lead, zinc, manganese, phosphates, antimony, bentonite, chromite, fluorospar, tungsten, limestone, gypsum, clay, sand and gravel, sapphires, garnets, agates, timber, grasslands

Business and Trade: Manufacturing, agriculture, mining, and tourism are Montana's principal industries. Almost four-fifths of the state's labor force work in service industries. Wholesale and retail businesses are the largest service-industry employers, accounting for about 19 percent of the gross state product (GSP—the annual value of all goods and services produced in the state) and 25 percent of Montana's workers. Government is the state's second-largest employer, accounting for 17 percent of the GSP and 26 percent of the state's employees. Montana's governmental service industries include military establishments, national parklands, and public schools. Community, social, and personal services such as private schools and hospitals, hotels, advertising and data processing services; transportation, communication, and utilities; and finance, insurance, and real estate are Montana's other important service industries. The remaining one-fifth of Montana's GSP comes from manufacturing, mining, construction, and agriculture.

Communication: Montana's first newspaper was the *Montana Post*, founded in Virginia City in 1864. More weekly papers quickly sprang up in other gold-mining camps. In the 1890s, W. A. Clark and Marcus Daly gained control of many of

Montana's major newspapers to ensure that their mining operations were presented in a favorable light. In 1959, the Anaconda Company sold the last of its newspaper holdings in Montana. Today, about 80 newspapers are published in Montana, 11 of them daily papers. Those with the largest circulations are the *Billings Gazette*, the *Great Falls Tribune*, and the *Missoulian*. Montana's first radio station was KFBB, which began broadcasting in 1922. Its first television stations were KXLF and KOPR, both of which began operating in Butte in 1953. Today, about 15 television stations and 95 radio stations broadcast in Montana.

Transportation: Transportation is important in Montana because products and people must travel such great distances to markets and other destinations. Montana's first railroad was the Utah & Northern, which began operation in the territory in 1880. In the following decade, two transcontinental railways began running through Montana: the Northern Pacific and the Great Northern. (They later combined to form the Burlington Northern.) The Chicago, Milwaukee, St. Paul & Pacific Railway completed its line through Montana in 1909. Today, Montana's freight and passenger trains run on about 3,480 mi. (5,600 km) of track. About three-fifths of Montana's 71,000 mi. (114,260 km) of roads are paved. Interstate 90 joins Interstate 94 to form an east-west route across the state. In the western part of the state, Interstate 15 is the major north-south route, passing through Butte, Helena, and Great Falls. The state highway system maintains excellent roads throughout the state. Air service began in Montana in 1928, when National Parks Airways began flying between Great Falls and Salt Lake City, Utah. Today, about 170 airports serve Montana's cities and towns. The airports at Billings, Bozeman, and Great Falls are the major commercial air facilities. A number of large farms in Montana have private airfields.

SOCIAL AND CULTURAL LIFE

Museums: The Montana Historical Society, in Helena, includes the Mackay Gallery of Charles Russell's paintings and sculptures and the Haynes Gallery of works by photographer F. Jay Haynes. It also features exhibits on twelve thousand years of Montana history. The C. M. Russell Museum, in Great Falls, features the works of Montana's beloved cowboy artist, as well as other Western history and art collections. Next to the museum are Russell's log-cabin studio and home. The Museum of the Plains Indian and Craft Center in Browning features an extensive collection of Blackfeet Indian artifacts and exhibits on the history and culture of the Northern Plains Indian tribes. The Museum of the Rockies, on the Montana State University campus in Bozeman, features the geology, archaeology, and history of the northern Rocky Mountain region. Among its attractions are exhibits of dinosaur fossils and a planetarium.

Several historic buildings, as well as Western culture and history exhibits, can be seen at Big Horn County Historical Museum in Hardin and at the Historical Museum at Fort Missoula. Custer Battlefield National Monument, near Hardin, and Big Hole National Battlefield, near Wisdom, also maintain historical museums. In

Billings are the Yellowstone Art Center, Western Heritage Center, Peter Yegen Museum, and the restored Moss Mansion. Fort Benton Museum recalls the town's days as a fur-trading post and a Missouri River navigation center. Miles City's Range Riders Museum and Pioneer Memorial Hall commemorate the history of Montana's range country.

In the former copper capital of Butte, a 1905 mining camp is recreated in the World Museum of Mining. The beautifully restored Daly Mansion in Hamilton was the home of copper king Marcus Daly and his wife, Margaret. The Conrad Mansion in Kalispell is the restored 1895 home of colorful pioneer C. E. Conrad, the city's founder. Antique Ford automobiles are featured at the Towe Antique Ford Collection in Deer Lodge. Also in Deer Lodge is the Montana Territorial Prison, now a museum. The McCone County Museum in Circle features collections on the area's history and wildlife. Other historical and cultural museums in the northeastern part of the state are located in Wolf Point, Glasgow, Malta, Poplar, Sidney, and Plentywood.

Libraries: There are about 125 public libraries in Montana. The Montana State Library in Helena features a computerized information system on Montana's natural resources and a book-loan program for the blind and the physically disabled. The Montana Historical Society Library and Archives contain the largest collection of Montana historical materials in the world. This includes a large map collection, almost all of the newspapers ever published in Montana, and over 2,500 volumes on the Plains cattle industry. Good collections on regional history can be found in the libraries of the University of Montana (UM) in Missoula and Montana State University (MSU) in Bozeman. UM also houses a fine law library, and MSU is noted for its agriculture and science collections. The Eastern Montana College library in Billings contains extensive materials on George Custer and the Battle of the Little Bighorn. Local history collections are also available at the libraries in Billings, Great Falls, Helena, Missoula, and Kalispell. The Montana State Law Library in Helena serves both state employees and the general public.

Performing Arts: The Billings Symphony Orchestra and Chorale offers an annual season of symphonic and choral music, as well as an annual pops concert. Missoula and Helena also support symphony orchestras, and Helena's municipal band presents concerts during the summer. Great Falls's Symphony Association sponsors spring and summer performances. The Cascade Quartet of Great Falls offers classical and contemporary string quartet works. The Yellowstone Chamber Players provide a concert series to audiences in Billings and also tour the state, performing diverse chamber works ranging from Baroque to contemporary styles. Composed entirely of children who play violin, the Dillon Junior Fiddlers Association presents concerts and musical revues.

Theater ensembles in the state include the Actors Theatre Montana of Billings; Daystar, a Native American folklore dance-drama ensemble based in Great Falls; and the physically vigorous Aleph Movement Theatre of Helena, which presents new-theater pieces. Polson's Port Polson Players perform comedies suitable for dinner theaters. Shakespeare in the Parks, based in Bozeman, is a professional touring company that performs Shakespearean comedies in full Elizabethan costume. The Montana Repertory Theatre, a professional theater company in residence at the University of Montana in Missoula, tours with plays by Montana's regional playwrights.

The Bozeman-based Montana Ballet Company presents both traditional ballet and contemporary dance, with a special commitment to the expression of Montana and Western culture. Earthen Fire Dance Theatre, also of Bozeman, is a contemporary experimental ensemble that combines dance with other artistic media, such as sculpture and poetry.

Summer music and theater events include the Bigfork Summer Playhouse, the Red Lodge Music Festival for high-school students, the University of Montana's Summer Festival of Performing Arts, Montana State University's Adult Chamber Music Festival, the Fort Peck Fine Arts Council's Summer Theatre, the Helena Jazz Festival, the International Dixieland Jazz Festival in Great Falls, the Veterans Day Dixieland Jazz Festival in Missoula, the Big Sky Music Festival, and the International Choral Festival sponsored by Missoula's Mendelssohn Club.

Some of the many organizations and agencies promoting the performing arts in Montana are the Montana Arts Council, the Montana Institute of the Arts, the Montana Committee for the Humanities, and the Montana Performing Arts Consortium. The Montana Arts Council, a state agency, sponsors an Artists in Schools/Communities program, awards grants for cultural projects, and encourages the arts through a number of other services.

Sports and Recreation: Montana's national and state parklands and recreation areas attract campers, fishermen, hunters, boaters, rock hunters, hikers, horseback riders, and wildlife watchers. In the Rocky Mountains of northwestern Montana is Glacier National Park. Its spectacular scenery includes more than fifty glaciers. Visitors can drive across the Continental Divide at Logan Pass on the Going-to-the-Sun Road. The park is the United States portion of Waterton-Glacier International Peace Park, which extends across the Canadian border into Alberta. Yellowstone National Park extends into Wyoming from south-central Montana. Three of Yellowstone's five entrances are in Montana. Bordering Yellowstone is the rugged Absaroka-Beartooth Wilderness, whose mountainous scenery can be experienced from horseback and foot trails. To the east, lying partly in Wyoming, is Bighorn Canyon National Recreation Area. There, Yellowtail Dam forms Bighorn Lake, whose surrounding area provides camping, boating, hiking, and other recreational opportunities.

Montana has eleven national forests: Beaverhead, Bitterroot, Custer, Deerlodge, Flathead, Gallatin, Helena, Kootenai, Lewis and Clark, Lolo, and Kaniksu. Montana's sixty state parks include Lewis and Clark Caverns, Giant Springs, Missouri Headwaters, Medicine Rocks, West Shore, and Wild Horse Island.

Sports fishermen in Montana fish for trout, salmon, whitefish, perch, bass, crappie, pike, sturgeon, catfish, and other species in dozens of rivers and lakes. Some of the best rivers for fishing are the Yellowstone, Missouri, Madison, Flathead, and Clark Fork rivers. There are hunting seasons for elk, deer, black bears, moose, antelope, mountain sheep, ducks, geese, grouse, and pheasant. Skiing is a favorite winter sport in Montana. Big Sky, Bridger Bowl, Big Mountain, Red Lodge Mountain, Blacktail Mountain, Montana Snow Bowl, and many other areas offer lift-accessible ski slopes.

At Custer Battlefield National Monument, stone markers point out where individual soldiers fell during the Battle of the Little Bighorn.

Montana has a number of old mining camps and ghost towns, notably Virginia City, which has been restored to resemble its boomtown days. In Nevada City are several buildings modeled after those in the town's mining days. Some of Montana's ghost towns are Maiden, Kendall, and Gilt Edge.

Historic Sites and Landmarks:

Big Hole Battlefield National Monument, west of Wisdom, is the site where United States Army troops attacked Chief Joseph's band of Nez Perce Indians in 1877.

Chief Joseph Battlefield, south of Chinook, is the site where Chief Joseph of the Nez Perce surrendered after a six-day battle with U.S. Army troops in 1877.

Custer Battlefield National Monument, in the Little Bighorn River Valley south of Hardin, is the site of the Sioux and Cheyenne victory over Lieutenant Colonel George Custer in 1876; the battle is periodically reenacted.

Fort Union Trading Post National Historic Site, at the North Dakota border near Sidney, is the site of the Missouri River's preeminent fur-trading post from the 1830s until the Civil War.

Grant-Kohrs Ranch National Historic Site, near Deer Lodge, was a huge nineteenth-century ranch. Covering 1,564 acres (633 hectares), the site includes the original Victorian mansion and thirty outbuildings.

Original Montana Governor's Mansion, in Helena, was built in 1885 and was the home of nine Montana governors between 1913 and 1959.

Rosebud Battlefield, north of Decker, is the site of the 1876 battle between the Sioux and General Crook's troops.

Virginia City, southwest of Bozeman, is a restored mining boomtown with over twenty historic buildings. The world's richest placer gold discovery was made there in 1863.

Other Interesting Places to Visit:

Bannack, west of Dillon, is the site of the first major gold discovery in Montana. Also Montana's first territorial capital, Bannack is now a ghost town whose mining-camp buildings still stand.

Billings Historic District, in Billings, includes the Carlin Hotel, with its theater pipe organ; and the Rex Hotel, built with the help of Buffalo Bill Cody.

Chief Plenty Coups State Historic Park, near Pryor, was the home and burial site of Chief Plenty Coups, the last chief of the Crow.

Fort Keogh, southwest of Miles City, was at one time the largest cavalry post in Montana. It was built after the Battle of the Little Bighorn and led to the founding of Miles City.

Fossil Beds, on Hell Creek north of Jordan, is the site where paleontologists discovered a nearly complete skeleton of the fierce, carnivorous Tyrannosaurus Rex.

Giant Springs, in Great Falls, is one of the largest springs in the world. Seen by Lewis and Clark in 1805, the springs produce 270,000 gal. (1,022,058 l) a minute, or about 390 million gal. (1.5 billion l) a day.

Glacier National Park, in northwest Montana, is a scenic wonderland of glaciers, lakes, streams, wildflowers, waterfalls, forests, and wildlife with nearly 1,000 mi. (1,609 km) of trails. Park visitors may cross the Continental Divide at Logan Pass on the 50-mi. (80-km) Going-to-the-Sun Road.

Lewis and Clark Caverns, east of Whitehall, is one of the largest limestone caverns in the Northwest.

Medicine Rocks, in the badlands near Ekalaka, is an area of strange sandstone rock formations where Indian hunters once called upon spirits.

Missouri River Headwaters State Park, near Three Forks, is the point where Lewis and Clark found that the Jefferson, Madison, and Gallatin rivers meet to form the Missouri River.

Visitors who enter Yellowstone National Park from Montana's North Entrance can easily visit the park's Mammoth Hot Spring's, just across the border in Wyoming.

Montana Territorial Prison, in Deer Lodge, is a castlelike stone building that served as the first territorial prison in the West.

National Bison Range, off U.S. 93 at Moiese, is the grazing ground for one of the last bison herds in the United States; the range may be surveyed by a self-guided automobile tour.

Old Fort Benton, at the Missouri riverfront in Fort Benton, includes a frontier trading post and blockhouse from the fort's days as a center of Missouri River commercial traffic.

Pictograph Cave State Historic Site, southeast of Billings, preserves the remains of a prehistoric culture that existed at the site 5,000 years ago.

Pompey's Pillar, east of Billings, is the massive sandstone pillar on which William Clark carved his signature in 1806 while on his expedition with Meriwether Lewis; Clark named the pillar after Sacagawea's son, whom he had nicknamed "Pomp," meaning "little chief."

St. Ignatius Mission Church, at St. Ignatius, is the mission church built by Jesuit missionaries in 1854; fifty-eight original murals adorn its walls and ceilings.

Yellowstone National Park, at the Wyoming border south of Livingston, is an area of erupting geysers and bubbling mineral pools, reachable from Montana at three points.

IMPORTANT DATES

c. 8000 B.C.—The Folsom culture flourishes in what is now Montana

c. 5000 B.C.—People of the Yuma culture begin to appear in Montana

c. 1000 B.C.—Montana's Late Hunter period begins

A.D. 1743—François and Louis Joseph de La Vérendrye explore the nothern Great Plains, spotting "shining mountains," believed to be Montana's Big Horn Mountains

1803—Eastern Montana, as part of the Louisiana Purchase, becomes United States territory

1805-06—Meriwether Lewis and William Clark travel through Montana on their expedition through the American Northwest

1807—Manuel Lisa builds Montana's first fur-trading post at the mouth of the Bighorn River; John Colter crosses the area of present-day Yellowstone National Park

1808—Canadian fur trader David Thompson, working for the British-owned North West Company, builds a post on the Kootenai River

1809—David Thompson establishes the North West Company's Salish House on the Clark Fork near Thompson Falls

1821—The North West Company merges with the Hudson's Bay Company

1822—Andrew Henry erects a trading post on the Yellowstone River

1824—Alexander Ross leads an expedition through Hell Gate Canyon near present-day Missoula

1829—The American Fur Company founds Fort Union near the mouth of the Yellowstone River

1841—Father Pierre-Jean De Smet founds St. Mary's Mission for the Salish Indians near Stevensville in the Bitterroot Valley

1846—In the Oregon Treaty, Great Britain relinquishes its claims to northwest Montana, setting the portion of the international boundary west of the Continental Divide at the 49th parallel

1847—The American Fur Company establishes Fort Benton

1853—General Isaac Stevens leads a railroad survey team through Montana

1854 — Father Adrian Hoecken builds St. Ignatius Mission near Flathead Lake in Mission Valley

1855 — General Stevens negotiates peace treaties with Salish and Blackfeet Indians

1857 — Gold is discovered on Gold Creek

1862 — John White discovers gold on Grasshopper Creek, sparking a gold rush to Bannack

1863 — Idaho Territory, including present-day Montana, is established; one of the world's richest placer gold discoveries is made at Alder Gulch, now Virginia City; John Mullan completes construction of a wagon road from Fort Walla Walla to Fort Benton; Bannack and Virginia City residents form vigilante bands to deal with bandits and outlaws

1864 — Montana Territory is created, with Bannack as the capital; gold is discovered at Last Chance Gulch, present-day Helena; John Bozeman leads the first wagon train over the Bozeman Trail

1865 — Territorial capital is moved from Bannack to Virginia City

1866 — Cattleman Nelson Story drives a herd of Texas longhorn cattle into Montana; Fort C. F. Smith is built to protect travelers on the Bozeman Trail from Indians

1872 — Congress establishes Yellowstone National Park, the nation's first national park

1875 — Territorial capital moves from Virginia City to Helena; William Farlin strikes silver at Butte; W. A. Clark opens the Travonia mine in Butte; Marcus Daly arrives in Montana

1876 — Sioux and Cheyenne Indians defeat George Custer in the Battle of the Little Bighorn; Sioux Indians under Crazy Horse defeat General Crook in the Battle of the Rosebud

1877 — Chief Joseph and the Nez Perce defeat General Gibbon in the Battle of the Big Hole but later surrender to army troops near the Bears Paw Mountains; Fort Missoula and Fort Custer are built

1880 — Utah & Northern Railroad enters Montana; silver outstrips gold as Montana's most important mineral

1881 — Marcus Daly opens a copper mine at Butte; the city of Helena is incorporated

1883 — The Northern Pacific Railway completes its transcontinental main line through Montana

A Centennial Cattle Drive was part of the festivities surrounding the celebration of Montana's centennial in 1989.

1884—Constitutional convention delegates draw up a constituion in Helena; Montana appeals to Congress for statehood

1886-87—A severe winter blizzard kills tens of thousands of cattle

1889—Montana becomes the forty-first state

1893—Montana State University at Missoula, Montana State College at Bozeman, Montana School of Mines at Butte, and State Normal College at Dillon are established

1894—Voters select Helena over Anaconda as Montana's state capital

1899—William A. Clark wins election to the U.S. Senate

1902—Montana's state capitol building is completed

1908—Iron Mountain's Superior Hotel originates the now nationwide practice of equipping hotel rooms with Gideon Bibles

1909—The Chicago, Milwaukee, St. Paul & Pacific Railroad is completed in Montana

1910—Congress establishes Glacier National Park

1913—Natural gas deposits are discovered near Glendive

1914—Montana labor unions decline as Butte mines adopt an "open-shop" (nonunion) plan

1916—Montana representative Jeannette Rankin becomes the first woman elected to the U.S. Congress

1917-20—Drought devastates Montana farms

1924 — Montana institutes a mining-license tax

1926 — W. A. Clark's Butte holdings are sold to the Anaconda Copper Mining Company

1929 — Several more years of drought begin

1933 — Many federal assistance, relief, and reclamation programs begin in Montana

1934 — Butte miners' strikes restore "closed-shop" status in the mines

1935 — Helena is hit by earthquakes

1940 — Construction of Fort Peck Dam is completed

1941 — Montana Congresswoman Jeannette Rankin is the only member of Congress to vote against U.S. entry into World War II

1951 — Oil production begins in the Williston Basin of eastern Montana and western North Dakota

1952 — Construction of Hungry Horse Dam is completed

1955 — Anaconda Aluminum Company opens a plant at Columbia Falls

1961 — The nation's largest intercontinental ballistic missile installation begins operating in Great Falls

1966 — Construction of Yellowtail Dam on the Bighorn River is completed

1972 — Montana voters approve a new state constitution

1975 — Libby Dam power plant on the Kootenai River begins operation

1985 — Montana's Science and Technology Alliance is formed to find new ways to use the state's raw materials

1989 — Montana celebrates its centennial

1991 — The U.S. government approves drilling on the Blackfeet Indian Reservation

IMPORTANT PEOPLE

John M. Bozeman (1835-1867), pioneer; opened a trail, known as the Bozeman Trail or Powder River road, that ran north from the Oregon Trail near Casper, Wyoming, into Montana (1864); frequent Indian attacks along the road gave it the name "Bloody Bozeman"; the town of Bozeman was named for him

Richard Brautigan (1933-1986), novelist and essayist; lived for many years near Livingston; first gained fame with his novel *Trout Fishing in America* (1967); also wrote *The Tokyo-Montana Express* (1980)

James (Jim) Bridger (1804-1881), pioneer, scout; went west as a fur trapper and mountain man in 1822; established Fort Bridger (1843); scouted for many traders and trappers in Montana in the 1800s

Martha Jane "Calamity Jane" Burke (1851-1903), frontierswoman; moved to Virginia City in 1865; was an army scout on Indian campaigns, a prospector, and an expert at shooting and riding; known for her rough manners and sharp tongue; at various times, lived in Billings, Harlowton, Big Timber, and Livingston; ran a restaurant in Castle in her later years

William Clark (1770-1838), soldier, explorer; explored the northwest regions of the Louisiana Purchase territory, including Montana, with Meriwether Lewis (1804-06); superintendent of Indian affairs for Louisiana Territory (1807-21)

William A. Clark (1839-1925), banker, mining industrialist; ran both silver- and copper-mining operations in Butte; longtime rival of fellow "copper king" Marcus Daly; succeeded in fight to make Helena the state capital; elected to the U.S. Senate in 1899, resigned under threat of investigation, and won the seat again in 1901

John Colter (1775?-1813), explorer; took part in the Lewis and Clark Expedition; while on Manuel Lisa's 1807 trapping expedition, was the first white person to travel through the Yellowstone Park region, nicknamed Colter's Hell from his descriptions

Gary Cooper (1901-1961), born in Helena; film actor; famous for portraying strong, romantic heroes; won Academy Awards for his performances in *Sergeant York* (1941) and *High Noon* (1952); other well-known films include *The Virginian*, *Mr. Deeds Goes to Town*, and *Meet John Doe*

CALAMITY JANE

WILLIAM A. CLARK

GARY COOPER

Marcus Daly (1841-1900), mining industrialist; began mining copper in Butte in 1880; in 1891, organized the Anaconda Mining Company, which later combined with other enterprises into the Amalgamated Copper Company; longtime "copper king" rival of mine owner William A. Clark

Ralph DeCamp (1858-1936), artist; lived in Helena from 1896 to 1924; known for his landscapes; several of his murals hang in the state capitol, including his best-known work, *Gates of the Mountains*

Pierre-Jean De Smet (1801-1873), Belgian Jesuit missionary; came to the U.S. in 1821; began his ministry to the Salish and Blackfeet Indians in 1841, often settling disputes between Indians and white settlers; was called "Black Robe" by the Indians

Ivan Doig (1939-   ), born in White Sulphur Springs; journalist, novelist; wrote of his experiences growing up in Montana in his 1978 novel *This House of Sky*, which was nominated for a National Book Award; *Dancing at the Rascal Fair* (1987) and *Ride with Me, Mariah Montana* (1990) complete his Montana historical trilogy

Alfred Bertram (A.B.) Guthrie, Jr. (1901-   ), novelist, short-story writer; grew up in Choteau; his novel *The Big Sky* (1947) is set in Montana; won a Pulitzer Prize in 1950 for his novel *The Way West* (1949); wrote the screenplay for the movie *Shane*

Dashiell Hammett (1894-1961), writer; as a detective for the Pinkerton Agency, spent time in Butte investigating activities of the Industrial Workers of the World (IWW) among striking miners; used his experiences in Montana as the basis for his first detective novel, *Red Harvest* (1929); other novels include *The Maltese Falcon* (1930) and *The Thin Man* (1932)

Richard Hugo (1923-1982), poet, essayist; joined the faculty of the University of Montana in 1962, where he ran the creative writing program; his works include the poetry collections *Lady in Kicking Horse Reservoir* and *Making Certain It Goes On*; and *The Real West Marginal Way*, a collection of autobiographical essays

Chet Huntley (1911-1974), born in Cardwell; television news anchor; longtime news anchor for the National Broadcasting Company (NBC); conceived and organized the recreational ski complex at Big Sky in the Gallatin River Canyon south of Bozeman

Will James (1892-1942), artist, writer; came to Montana in 1910 to work as a cowboy; later lived and worked in Pryor on the Crow Reservation; a self-taught artist, he was inspired by Charles M. Russell; his own illustrations appear in his novels, which include *Cowboys North and South* (1924), *Smoky* (1926), and *Lone Cowboy* (1930)

MARCUS DALY

PIERRE-JEAN DE SMET

DASHIELL HAMMETT

CHET HUNTLEY

DOROTHY JOHNSON

CHIEF JOSEPH

MYRNA LOY

MIKE MANSFIELD

Dorothy M. Johnson (1905-1984), editor, short-story writer; grew up in Whitefish; her short stories "A Man Called Horse," "The Hanging Tree," and "The Man Who Shot Liberty Valance" were made into motion pictures

Chief Joseph (1840?-1904), Nez Perce Indian leader; born in the Wallowa Valley, Oregon, and became Nez Perce chief in 1871; led his people in resisting their removal from Oregon to an Idaho reservation; defeated army troops in several battles in Montana while leading his people toward Canada; surrendered to General Nelson A. Miles on October 5, 1877

William Kittredge (1932-   ), novelist, short-story writer; professor of English at the University of Montana (1969-   ), where he directs the creative writing program; his works include the short-story collections *Van Gogh Field* (1979), *We Are Not in This Together* (1984), and *Owning It All* (1987)

Meriwether Lewis (1774-1809), explorer; secretary to President Thomas Jefferson (1801-03); with William Clark, made the first systematic exploration of Montana while exploring and mapping the Northwest (1804-06); governor of Louisiana Territory (1807-09)

Manuel Lisa (1772-1820), fur trader; led a trading expedition up the Yellowstone River (1805) to the mouth of the Big Horn River, where he built Montana's first trading post (1807); also explored the upper Missouri River region, establishing several trading posts

Myrna Loy (1905-   ), born in Helena; actress; appeared in many films, including *The Thin Man* and several other "Thin Man" movies, *The Best Years of Our Lives*, and *Cheaper by the Dozen*

Norman Fitzroy Maclean (1902-1990), writer, educator; grew up in Missoula; professor of English literature at the University of Chicago; his experiences in Montana inspired many of his works, such as those in his collection *A River Runs Through It and Other Stories* (1976)

Michael Joseph (Mike) Mansfield (1903-   ), politician; Montana's most distinguished member of Congress; was born in New York City and moved to Montana at the age of three; worked as a miner and mining engineer in Butte mines (1922-31); professor of history and political science at the University of Montana (1933-42); U.S. representative from Montana (1943-53); U.S. senator (1953-77); served the longest term in history as Senate majority leader (1961-76); while in Congress, he opposed the Vietnam War, fought to pass the 1964 Civil Rights Act, and labored to lower the voting age to eighteen; U.S. ambassador to Japan (1977-89)

Thomas Francis McGuane III (1939-   ), novelist, screenwriter; lived near Livingston; his novels and screenplays include *Ninety-Two in the Shade*, *Rancho Deluxe*, *Tom Horn*, and *Missouri Breaks*

Plenty Coups (1848-1933), born near Billings; Crow Indian leader; worked as a scout for the U.S. Army; in 1921, represented American Indians at the dedication ceremony for the Tomb of the Unknown Soldier in Arlington, Virginia, where he delivered a moving speech on war and peace; his home and burial place are in Pryor on the Crow Reservation

Jeannette Rankin (1880-1973), born near Missoula; politician, social reformer; active in woman-suffrage movement; as a U.S. representative from Montana (1917-19, 1941-43); was the first woman ever to hold a seat in the U.S. Congress; was the only member of Congress to vote against U.S. entry into both World War I (1917) and World War II (1941); opposed American intervention in Vietnam

JEANNETTE RANKIN

Charles Marion Russell (1864-1926), artist; moved to Montana at the age of sixteen and worked for years as a cowboy; recorded his observations in thousands of drawings and paintings of cowboy and Indian life and Western landscapes; wrote a collection of cowboy stories entitled *Trails Plowed Under* (1937)

Sacagawea (1786?-1812?), Shoshone Indian interpreter and guide; probably born near Lemhi, Idaho; captured in 1800 and sold to Toussaint Charbonneau, a Canadian trapper, whom she married in 1804; with her husband, joined the Lewis and Clark Expedition in 1805 and served as a guide

CHARLES M. RUSSELL

Wallace Earle Stegner (1909-   ), novelist, short-story writer; lived in Montana as a child; received the 1972 Pulitzer Prize in fiction for his novel *Angle of Repose*, received a National Book Award for *The Spectator Bird*

David Thompson (1770-1857), explorer, fur trader; worked for Britain's Hudson's Bay Company (1784-97) and North West Company (1797-1836); from 1789 to 1812, explored and mapped western Canada and the American Northwest; first white person to explore the entire course of the Columbia River; in 1809, established Salish House on the Clark Fork near Thompson Falls, which are named for him

LESTER THUROW

Lester Carl Thurow (1938-   ), born in Livingston; economist; professor at Harvard University (1965-68); served on the faculty of Massachusetts Institute of Technology, where he was dean of the school of management; member of the editorial board of the *New York Times* (1979) and contributing editor of *Newsweek* magazine (1981); wrote several books on economics

Harold Clayton Urey (1893-1981), chemist and atomic energy researcher; grew up in Montana and graduated from the University of Montana; professor at Columbia University, the University of Chicago, and the University of California, La Jolla; discovered heavy water, helped develop the atomic bomb, and studied the origins of the planets; received the 1934 Nobel Prize in chemistry for discovering heavy hydrogen

HAROLD UREY

THOMAS WALSH

Thomas James Walsh (1859-1933), lawyer, politician; began practicing law in Helena in 1890; U.S. senator from Montana (1913-33); as a senator, led the investigation of the Teapot Dome scandal (1923); appointed U.S. attorney general by President Franklin Roosevelt, he died before taking office; first Montanan named to a cabinet post

James Welch (1940-   ), born in Browning; novelist, poet; son of Blackfeet and Gros Ventre parents, he grew up on the Blackfeet and Fort Belknap reservations; taught at the University of Washington and Cornell University; evoked the beauty and dignity of his native people in his poetry collection *Riding the Earthboy 40* (1971) and his novels *Winter in the Blood* (1974), *The Death of Jim Loney* (1979), and *Fools Crow* (1986)

Burton Kendall Wheeler (1882-1975), politician; U.S. senator from Montana (1923-47); ran for vice-president on the Progressive party ticket with Robert M. LaFollette in 1924

GOVERNORS

Joseph K. Toole	1889-1893
John E. Rickards	1893-1897
Robert Burns Smith	1897-1901
Joseph K. Toole	1901-1908
Edwin L. Norris	1908-1913
Sam V. Stewart	1913-1921
Joseph M. Dixon	1921-1925
John E. Erickson	1925-1933
Frank H. Cooney	1933-1935
W. Elmer Holt	1935-1937
Roy E. Ayers	1937-1941
Sam C. Ford	1941-1949
John W. Bonner	1949-1953
J. Hugo Aronson	1953-1961
Donald G. Nutter	1961-1962
Tim M. Babcock	1962-1969
Forrest H. Anderson	1969-1973
Thomas L. Judge	1973-1981
Ted Schwinden	1981-1989
Stan Stephens	1989-1993
Mark Racicot	1993-

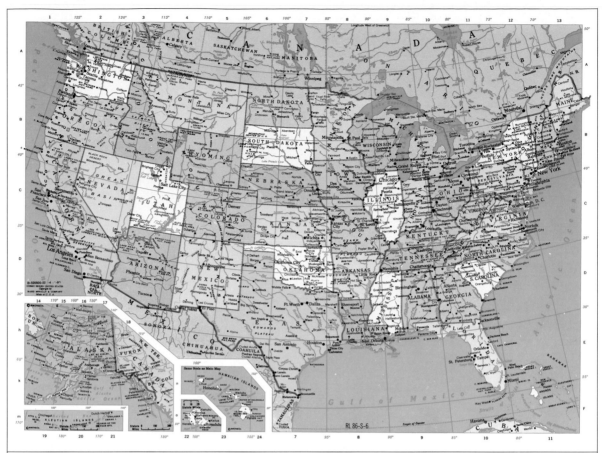

Topography

MAP KEY

From *Cosmopolitan World Atlas* © 1990 by Rand McNally, R.L. 90-S-252

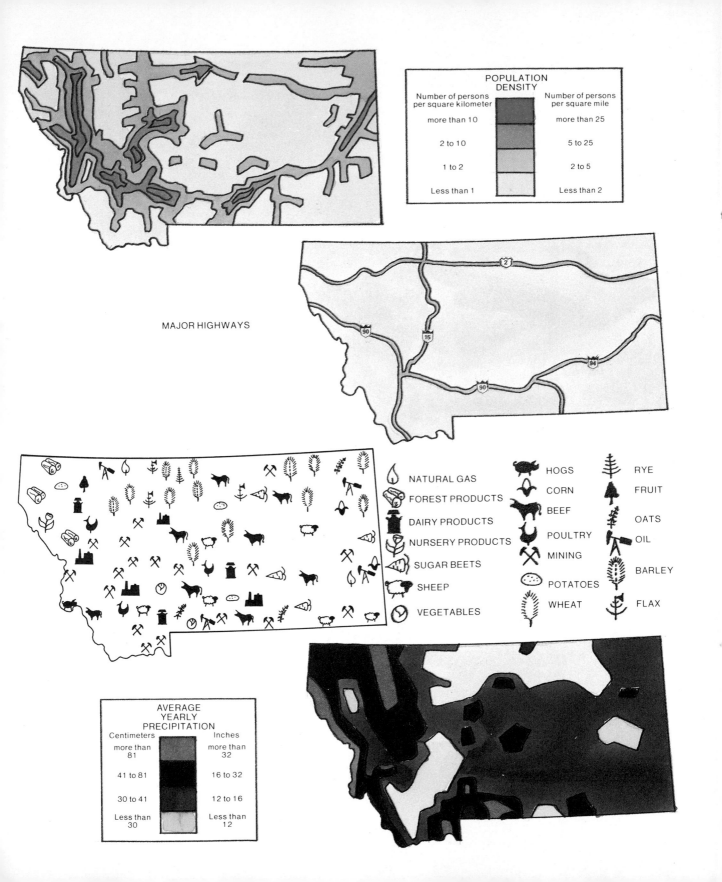

POPULATION
DENSITY

Number of persons per square kilometer		Number of persons per square mile
more than 10		more than 25
2 to 10		5 to 25
1 to 2		2 to 5
Less than 1		Less than 2

MAJOR HIGHWAYS

NATURAL GAS

FOREST PRODUCTS

DAIRY PRODUCTS

NURSERY PRODUCTS

SUGAR BEETS

SHEEP

VEGETABLES

HOGS

CORN

BEEF

POULTRY

MINING

POTATOES

WHEAT

RYE

FRUIT

OATS

OIL

BARLEY

FLAX

AVERAGE
YEARLY
PRECIPITATION

Centimeters		Inches
more than 81		more than 32
41 to 81		16 to 32
30 to 41		12 to 16
Less than 30		Less than 12

TOPOGRAPHY

Courtesy of Hammond, Incorporated
Maplewood, New Jersey

COUNTIES

Sinopah Mountain, Glacier National Park

INDEX

Page numbers that appear in boldface type indicate illustrations

Members of the Madison County Side Saddle Club participating in an Ennis rodeo

Picture Identifications
Front cover: Mount Gould from Swiftcurrent Lake, Glacier National Park
Pages 2-3: Rainbow over St. Ignatius Mission
Page 6: Glacier National Park
Pages 8-9: The Yellowstone River Valley
Pages 18-19: Montage of Montana residents
Pages 26-27: *When Blackfeet and Sioux Meet*, by Charles M. Russell
Pages 34-35: *Custer's Last Stand*, by Edgar Paxson
Pages 50-51: A photograph from the early 1900s of tourists at Glacier National Park
Page 60: The Montana State Capitol in Helena
Pages 72-73: Horseback riding in northwestern Montana
Pages 84-85: The Garden Wall, Glacier National Park
Page 108: Montage of state symbols, including the state flag, state tree (ponderosa pine), state animal (grizzly bear), state flower (bitterroot), and state bird (western meadowlark)
Back cover: An old homestead on Montana's Great Plains

Picture Acknowledgments

About the Author

Ann Heinrichs is a free-lance writer and editor living in Chicago. She has worked for such educational publishers as Encyclopaedia Britannica, World Book Encyclopedia, and Science Research Associates. As a music critic and feature writer, her articles have appeared in various publications. She is the author of a number of books, including several in the *America the Beautiful* series. Mystified by the wide-open spaces of the West, she heads out that way whenever she can.